ANCIENT EGYPT

A Simple Walkthrough

By Keith Ellis

Ancient Egypt

A Simple Walkthrough

Copyright © 2014 Keith Ellis. All rights reserved.
First paperback edition printed 2014 in the United Kingdom.

No part of this book shall be reproduced or transmitted in any form or by any means, electronic or mechanical, including photocopying, recording, or by any information retrieval system without written permission of the publisher.

Published by Compass Publishing
More copies of this book available from
www.asimplewalkthrough.com
www.asimplewalkthrough.co.uk

Contains over 130 colour photos

Acknowledgement

My Children, Kayleigh and Greg

My partner Karen

My Father Ron (for buying a daily newspaper)

Cover Pictures: The Sphinx and Great Pyramid of Giza.

Although every precaution has been taken in the preparation of this book, the publisher and author assume no responsibility for errors or omissions. Neither is any liability assumed for damages resulting from the use of this information contained herein.

ISBN 978-1-907308-91-8

Authors note

Having read hundreds of books, thousands of pages, sat through countless documentaries and visited Egypt twice, (and wished I had been an archaeologist since a boy) I wanted to create something for everyone.
A simple walk through the pages, interesting articles, main places and people of their times and hopefully a book you will enjoy, whether it be your first or last Ancient Egyptian experience.

Contents

Early Egypt and the first settlers.
The Nile, a gift from the Gods. King Narmer unites two lands.
The Nileometer and the yearly floods.

Chapter 2

Ancient Egyptians and Religion. Important Gods & Goddesses.
Mummification and the Afterlife.

Chapter 3

Ancient Egyptian writing. Hieroglyphs and the discovery
of the Rosetta stone.
Papyrus, Scribes and Education.

Chapter 4

Every day life of Ancient Egyptians. Farming & brewing beer.
Medicine & hygiene. Perfume, cosmetics & clothing.
Toys, games and family pets.

Chapter 5

A look at the most important Cities & Temples along the Nile.
From Alexandria on the Mediterranean to Abu Simbel, 1485km (922miles) away on the borders of
Sudan.

Chapter 6

The Pharaohs.
The most powerful and influential Kings of ancient Egypt, spanning over 3000 years.
The Queens of Ancient Egypt

Chapter 7
Present day Egypt

Preface

One day, as a ten year old boy in 1972, I dragged myself out of bed after my mother had called me numerous times to get up and ready for school.
I went down stairs for my breakfast, probably to dress as in those days there was no central heating and we dressed in front of an open fire.
My father was a lorry driver who worked shifts; he had arrived home earlier and retired to bed. On the dining table was his daily paper and on the front page was the headline announcing the arrival of the treasures of Tutankhamun in England, to be displayed at the London Museum.

There, below the headline was a full page picture of the golden death mask of Tutankhamun.
I stared into his eyes for what seemed like an age before reading the article.
Here was a young boy who had become Pharaoh at the age of ten, my age;
King of Ancient Egypt with the whole of the Egyptian empire on his shoulders.
All I had to think about was which cereals to have for breakfast.

From that day, I was captivated. I drew a picture of the golden mask at school that won first prize at a local annual fair,
I read countless books and when birthdays and Christmases came around I asked for Ancient Egypt related presents.

I did not visit Egypt, however, until I was 39, when I cruised the Nile from Luxor to Aswan. In 2012 I returned for another cruise, but this time finished my holiday with a flight to Cairo. There I visited the Cairo Museum and finally came face to face with the golden Mask.
I stood there, staring into those eyes as I had done years before. The only difference being that this time I understood about the boy King and his short life.
I took a deep breath as a lump entered my throat and those eyes gazed back; lifeless, yet saying so much.

Chapter 1

Page 6. Reference Map
Page 7. The Nile
Page 8. Early Egypt
Page 9. Nileometer

Right: This picture, taken by the author in 2012 from a Nile cruise boat, shows the river extending for miles ahead. The Nile is 4,132 miles (6,650km) long.

Left: Trees flourish along the Nile close to the desert due to rich silts deposited by the floods over thousands of years and the use of inland water channels and irrigation.

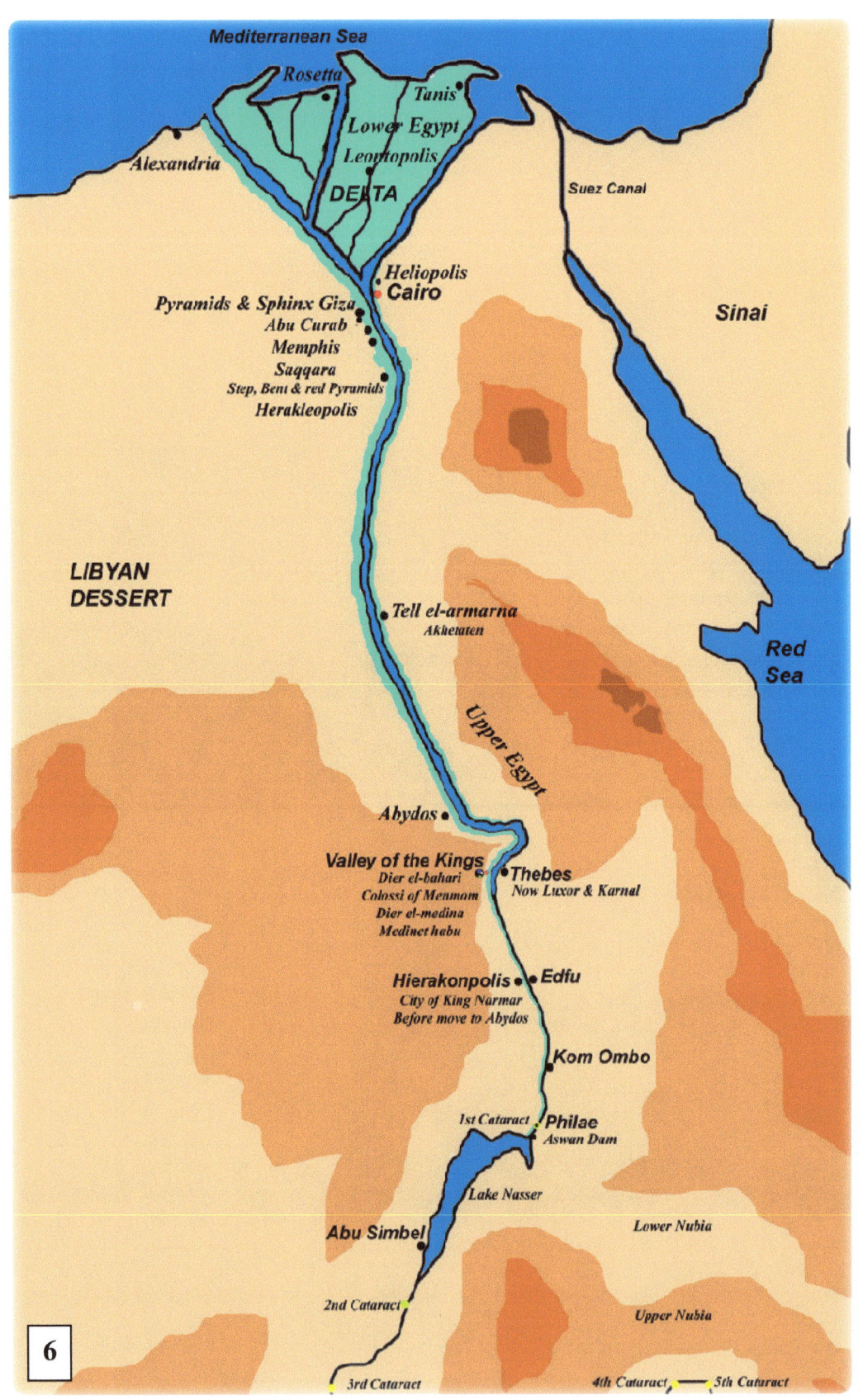

The Nile
A gift from the Gods

The Nile originates in the highlands of Uganda and Ethiopia. These two rivers are known as the Blue and the White Nile. They join into a single flow at Khartoum in Sudan, then carry on Northwards over a series of cataracts *(set of rapids)* through the Nubian Desert, before forming the Egyptian Nile.

Without the Nile, which irrigates the land each side of its banks with yearly floods and opens into a vast Delta before meeting the Mediterranean, Egypt would be a huge desert.

This picture, taken from a boat by the author, shows how close the edge of the desert is to the Nile waters in some places.

The Egyptians were totally dependent on the Nile and its annual floods. Each year the waters would deposit rich silt onto the soil of the fields. It was the main communication route through the country and supplied them with fish, waterfowl, reeds for baskets, mud for pottery and bricks and papyrus for paper.

The entire way of life in ancient Egypt was dependent on the Nile. Flooding would start around June and continue until September. The fields could not be worked at this time, so most of the labour was used on the building of Temples and Monuments. They returned to cultivate the earth, now fertilised by new silt deposits around November for the following year.

The level of the Nile was recorded on an ancient Egyptian invention called a Nileometer *(page 9)*. This was usually in the form of marked steps at the bank against which the changing levels could be watched. Others such as the ones in Temples would be underground fed, through tunnels leading into a well. Old records could be used each year to estimate the final height of the water. With this they could move to higher grounds in the best years, even telling how far inland the water would spread. In the years of low levels, food would be stored in case of periods of drought and to limit famine.

Early Egypt

Between 8000 and 5000 BC, a flow of people from Asia and Africa entered Upper and Lower Egypt. Slowly, the immense forests and endless lagoons disappeared as a radical change came to this part of the world. The desert closed in and endless flood tides of the great river Nile left muddy bogs along its banks.

The 4th millennium then witnessed the development of an extraordinary group of people who mastered the art of regulating the muddy water along miles of riverbank, co-ordinating agricultural activities across thousands of hectares and creating villages and cities.

This was the beginning of the most extensive organised society that ever existed.

Lower Egypt spread out amongst 150 miles of countless delta rivers by the Mediterranean. Upper Egypt, south of Cairo, flanked the Nile for hundreds of miles. These people turned their attention to internal problems when they began to produce less and less from their lands.

Lower Egypt had its own problems. With the ever-growing trade from the Mediterranean came wealth and power. This brought about conflicts and religious differences (*Chapter 2*).

Finally King Narmer of Nekham Upper Egypt moved his capital to Abydos, nearer to Lower Egypt and invaded lands right up to the Mediterranean. The ten leading citizens were beheaded.

Narmer placed the red crown of Lower Egypt on his head.

The first dynasty of absolute power had begun.

The Three Crowns

The picture below shows the different crowns of Narmer. His own white crown of Upper Egypt placed with the red crown of Lower to become the symbol of united Egypt.

Nileometer

Egyptian life was very dependent on the flooding of the Nile. With very low rain fall in Egypt the Nile was used to irrigate the lands.

At the start of the summer the Egyptians would begin to record levels of the river using a Nileometer. These were wells built alongside the river bank, they had stairways that led down to the water but also acted as a scale for measuring the water levels.

Each step was one cubit high (52.4cm). Some Nileometers, such as the one at Karnak, were fed by tunnels because they were not near the bank.

Levels of the floods were recorded in royal records and very high or low levels would be marked on the walls of the Nileometer.

Officials could work out how far the water would spread inland and decide which fields would be used and if reserves of grain were needed in bad years.

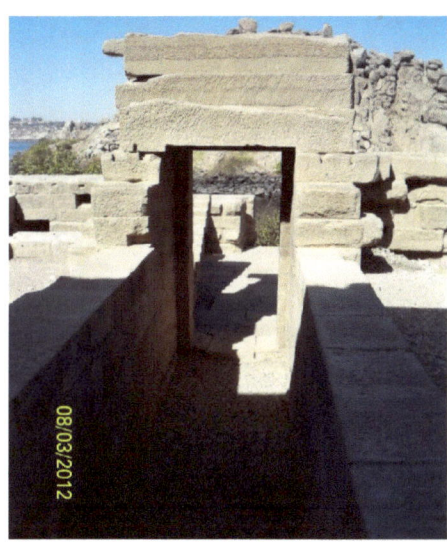 

Left: Opening leading to steps of Nileometer at the Temple of Philae.
Right: A well with steps at the Temple of KomOmbo.

An Ancient Egyptian Cubit was a measurement from the Elbow to the tip of the middle finger.

Chapter 2

Page 11. Religion
Page 12. Horus
Page 13. Gods & Goddesses
Page 14. Gods & Goddesses (In Form)
Page 15. Mummification
Page 16. Anubis
Page 17. Canopic jars
Page 18. Sarcophagus
Page 19. Journey to the afterlife
Page 20. The Ankh

Religion

Gods and Goddesses

Egyptians believed that Nun, the eternal ocean, filled the universe. After the waters subsided, the sun God Atum, the creator God, was standing upon a hill. Atum created 2 children, Shu (air) and Tefnut (moisture). These created Geb (earth) and Nut (sky).
Geb and Nut created 4 children, Osiris, Seth, Isis and Nephthys.

Osiris

The most worshipped god of the Egyptians. In the world of the dead he ruled over the court that judged the earthly acts of the dead. With the weighing of the deceased's heart he would determine if they won eternal bliss or were condemned to damnation. He wears the plumed crown and holds the crook for guiding his people and the whip (flail) that symbolised authority.

Isis

Isis was sister and wife of Osiris, and mother of their son Horus. With the creative forces of Osiris and Isis also came the destructive forces of Seth, brother of Osiris and Nephthys, aide to Isis. Seth is jealous of Osiris and kills him. Isis resurrects him with the help of her son and the god Anubis. She is therefore seen as the goddess of all living creatures. The emblem she wears on her head is the symbol for throne, symbolising her role as mother of all Egyptian rulers.

Horus

Above: statue of Horus at Edfu Temple.

Ruler and protector of the living, Horus was the son of Osiris and Isis. His father was killed by his envious uncle Seth. In a battle lasting 80 years, Horus defeats Seth but loses an eye which becomes known as the Wedjet eye (*see below*).

After his victory over Seth, Horus becomes the God of the sky and protector of the Pharaohs. During life the Pharaoh was linked to Horus but after death he was associated with Osiris.

Left: The Wedjet eye, Kom Ombo Temple.

The eye was found by his mother and restored by the Goddess Hathor. Being the sky God the eye represented the sun and the moon, but was also used to symbolise healing and protection. It could also combat evil and was depicted on the tombs for the deceased to observe the outside world

Right: Horus wearing the double crown, Kom Ombo. (*See page 8*).

Gods and Goddesses

Name	Form	Task
Atum	Man	First creator
RA-light and conscience	Solar Disc	Tears, human life.
Amon-spirit of universe	Ram/Feather crown	Words, divine creatures.
Tefnut	Lion	Moisture
Shu	Greatfeather	Air.
Geb		Earth.
Nut	Stars	Sky.
Osiris	Man	Seed of life / Protector of afterlife.
Isis	Woman	Love of creatures.
Horus	Falcon	Ruler of living
Hathor	Solar disc/cow	Love/Music/Dance
Seth	Monstrous animal	Destruction

Use these two pages for reference when you come across a God or Goddess later on in the book.

Nephthys	Tower/pillar	Aid to Isis
Nekhbet	Vulture	Protector of royal children
Ptah	Mummified man	God of city Memphis
Sekhmet	Lioness	Destroys enemies of RA
Maat	Ostrich Feather	Ethical values and justice
Thoth	Ibis	Teacher, writing/wisdom
Sobek	Crocodile	God of water/Nile
Khnum	Ram	Potter, sculpture of mans form
Khepri	Scarab	Rising of the sun

Gods & Goddesses (In Form)

It should be noted that a God or Goddess could be worshipped in the form of a statue or the incarnation of an animal. Egyptians considered all form of life to be an expression of the divine RA. Every animal was sacred, a human image or statue did not take preference over his animal form.

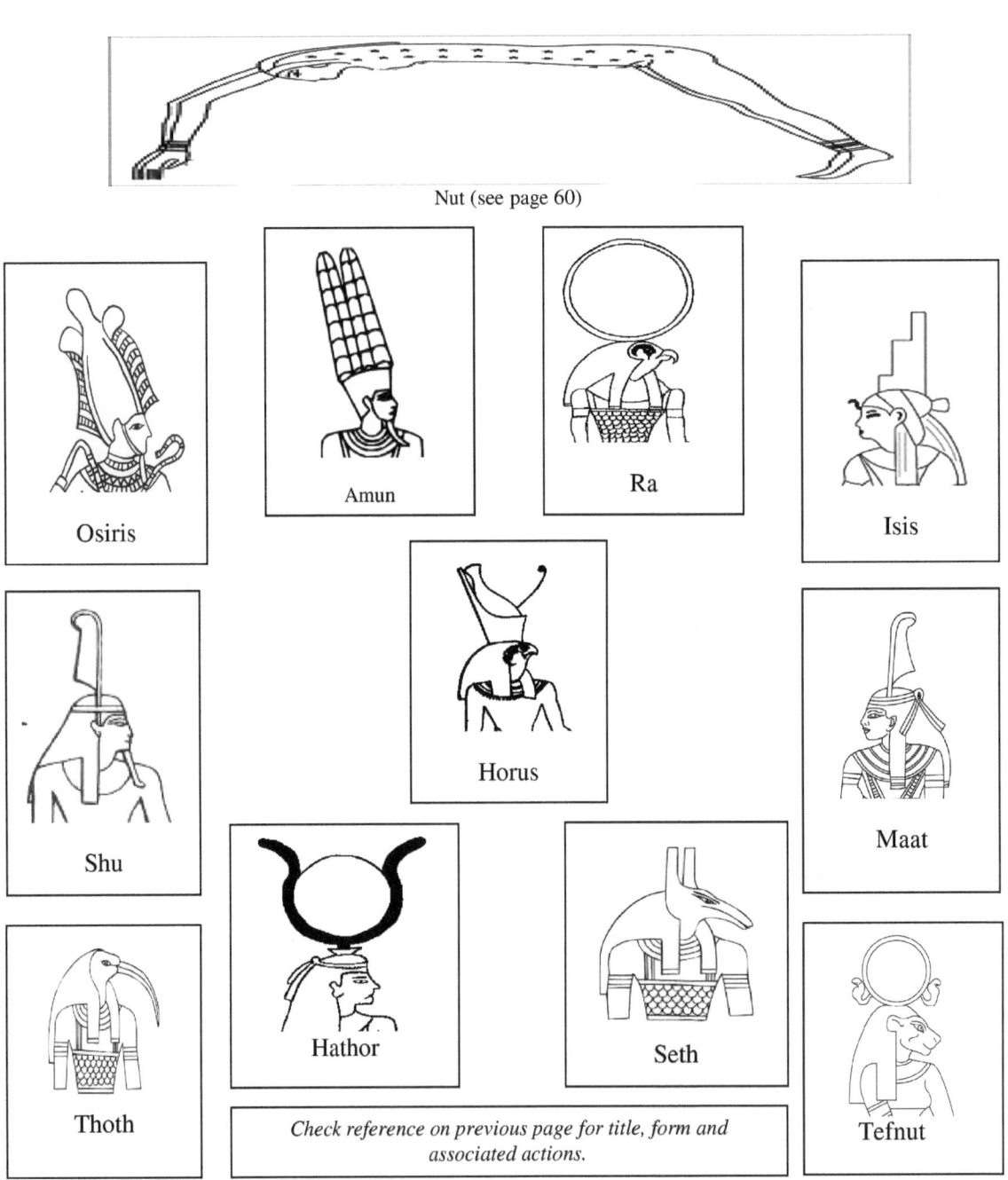

Nut (see page 60)

Osiris | Amun | Ra | Isis

Shu | Horus | Maat

Thoth | Hathor | Seth | Tefnut

Check reference on previous page for title, form and associated actions.

Mummification

Egyptians believed that the preserving of the body let the soul journey to the next life. In early burials people were placed in the foetal position (like a baby in the mothers womb), sewn into animal skins and encased in clay. They would then be buried in the sand and the body would quickly dehydrate and preserve. This was later used on common people, but the most expensive procedure was mummification. This lasted up to 70 days and was used on high officials and the pharaoh.

During the funerary rites, a priest would wear the black Jackal Mask of Anubis.

The body was taken to the house of purification and placed in a tent called an 'Ibu'. After being washed, the stomach intestines, lungs and liver were removed.
The brain was removed through the nose with a long hook and all organs were placed in canopic jars. The heart was covered with a wooden carving of Khepri. *(see below.)*
The body was then stuffed and covered in Natron; a natural salt, and left to dry out. After this the body was washed and oils were rubbed into the skin to keep it elastic. During the process of bandaging, many charms and amulets were placed between the layers for protection in the next world. Priests would read from the book of the dead and finally slits were made at the eyes and mouth. The pharaoh must be able to speak and see in the next life.
The word Mummification comes from the Latin word 'Mumia'. This was black bitumen used in later dynasties instead of balsam and resins.

Right: (Scarab) Khepri the scarab beetle was foremost among sacred creatures.
Used as a hieroglyph it expressed the concept of becoming and being.
The Egyptians believed the beetle would emerge from the ground in the morning and carry the sun across the sky. Returning to the ground at night.
It was also unlucky to crush one.
The Scarab in this picture is from the Temple of Karnak from the time of Amenhotep III and represents the rising sun.

Anubis

Weighing of the Heart

Anubis was probably one of the most important Gods for the Egyptians in death.
The Jackal headed God would guide the deceased to the underworld and take part in the judging and weighing of the heart for the journey to the afterlife (See page 19).
Having played an important part in the resurrection of Osiris, Anubis became known as the God of Mummification.
The worship of Anubis can be traced back to Early Egyptian history; being associated with the dead he was worshiped all over Egypt.

Pic 1

Pic 2

Anubis is a striking figure with his black jackal head. Seen on many tomb walls, often receiving the dead or in the ceremony of opening the mouth (*Pic 2*). The Egyptians believed the soul would have to eat, drink, breath and speak in the afterlife.
In picture 1 Anubis is seen at the weighing of the heart. Black was a reference to the putrefying corpse but also the black soil of the Nile which symbolised rebirth.

Canopic jars

As the Ancient Egyptians believed in the afterlife, great care was taken to preserve not only the body but the organs as well. They were removed from the body and treated before being placed in vases that became known as Canopic jars. The name comes from the town of Canopus near Alexandria, were human headed jars were worshipped in the image of Osiris.

Qebehseneuf   Duamutef   Hapy   Imsety

Each jar had the head of one of the four sons of Horus to protect the organs. The sons were themselves protected by four deities, guarding the main points of the compass.
Qebehsenuef, the falcon headed jar, guarded the intestines and was linked to the Goddess Serket who protected the West.
Hapy, the ape headed jar, was linked with the Goddess Nephthys of the North and protected the lungs.
Duamutef the jackal protected the stomach and the Goddess Neith gave support from the East.
Imsety with the human head guarded the liver and was linked with the goddess Isis and the South.

The alabaster lids of the Canopic jars from the tomb of the boy Pharaoh, Tutankhamun. Here they represent the King himself instead of the sons of Horus. It is probably because his father, Akhenatan, (*p75*) changed the religious culture to one God that the lids are in the form of the boy King and not other Gods.
18th Dynasty 1334-1325
Egyptian Museum, Cairo.

Sarcophagus

After the mummification process, the body was then taken to the burial site. The resting place of high-ranking Egyptians was essential for eternal life.
(See Tombs and Pyramids p55).

It was then placed into the sarcophagus *(coffin)*, which protected the deceased without shutting him off from the outside world. This was very important, especially for the dead pharaoh, whose duty of looking over his people continued even in the afterlife. Wood or terracotta replaced the first basket sarcophagi. Later, towards the end of the New Kingdom, they were skilfully crafted inside and out and beautifully decorated, often being made completely of gold.

Those of the pharaohs' were the most magnificent and sometimes consisted of several fitted one inside the other, carved with features to represent the pharaoh within.

Sadly, most sarcophagi were plundered by grave robbers over centuries and the mummy was usually thrown out and cast aside after being robbed of the jewellery and amulets placed in with it at the time of burial.

Amenhotep II. *(Shown above)* was the first of only two pharaohs found still in their sarcophagus. His body was removed in 1928 and placed on show in the Cairo Museum. The second - and probably most famous pharaoh named today - was the boy king Tutankhamun.

Although he is well known today, Tutankhamun was relatively a minor pharaoh who reigned for a short period. We can only wonder then what some of the other great pharaohs' sarcophagi could have looked like.

The sarcophagus was placed in one of the many chambers at the burial site and more about these chambers can be found in the section relating to Tutankhamun.

Here we will also see more of his magnificent sarcophagus. But now we will look at the pharaoh's journey to the afterlife.

Journey to the afterlife

Khet was the name given to the human body and KA was the spiritual body. Together they gave rise to the soul, which the Egyptians called BA.
There was no break between the realms of earth and the afterworld, death would be the release of BA and the beginning of its journey to the afterlife.
The funeral rites and the cult of the dead assumed maximum importance and were available to all, but the pharaoh was the most important. Seen as the earthly body of God, his actions as absolute father and protector continued after death. The journey itself would be full of tests and dangers, and the BA was guided and protected by Anubis. Scrolls would be placed next to the body containing text from the book of the dead. This was a very important book to the Egyptians, but it was not looked upon as a bible. It was a collection of funeral spells and hymns to the Gods to ensure safety in the next life. The book was also a kind of map or guide to the right roads to take on the journey.

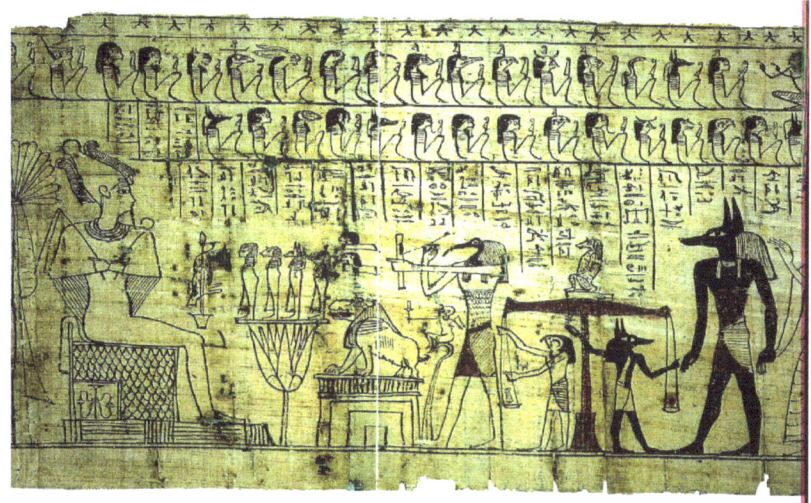

The journey would begin at the western mountain, the gate to the next world. Here the deceased would board the celestial boat, the Solar barge and descend to the river in the 'gallery of night'; the gloomy realm of Seth.
Here the enemies of Osiris would try to block the way. Next they came to the seven gates of exit watched over by the Gods of magic, questions and the guardian God. The soul had to pass a test to continue to the passage of ten pylons. Then the soul would arrive in the Hall of justice for the weighing of the heart. If the heart was as light as a feather, the soul could continue to the Lotus Lake and everlasting life in the fields of Yalu.

Picture: Anubis (*far right*) weighs the heart watched over by Osiris (*far left*) and helped by Thoth, the Ibis headed God of writing and wisdom. If the heart was too heavy, Ammut the devourer (*centre on pedestal*) would eat it. The deceased would be condemned to eternal death.

The Ankh

The Ankh is one of the most commonly known Egyptian symbols. It is also called the key of life and is the hieroglyphic symbol for life. Tomb paintings often show the God or Goddess holding the Ankh as a gift of life to the dead person's mummified body.

Being the symbol of life, the Ankh was and still is worn around the neck as a protective amulet. In modern Egypt many caretakers of monuments and temples carry the key with the handle in the shape of an Ankh. (*Pic 2*)

The Ankh was also often held in the hands of the Pharaohs on their statues as the king was protector of the people's lives.

There are many disputes about what the shape represents. Some archaeologists even think it is a symbol of an ancient Egyptian sandal. But the most popular belief is the Ankh being a symbol of sunrise.
The top represents the sun, the crossbar the horizon and the bottom vertical bar the path of the sun. (*Pic 1*)

Pic 1

Below: The author and his family at the entrance to Abu Simbel showing the caretakers key shaped as an Ankh.

Pic 2

Chapter 3

Page 22. Hieroglyphs
Page 23. Hieroglyphs explained
Page 24. The Rosetta Stone
Page 25. Scribes
Page 26. Papyrus
Page 27. Education

Hieroglyphs

The Ancient Egyptians used objects of everyday life to create their writing. The animals, plants, natural elements, household objects and buildings were transformed into hieroglyphs.

The biggest sections are those of the human body, but animals and birds play an important part. Other groups include tools, weapons, boats, crowns and jewels.

The only Egyptians that knew how to read and write were royalty, civil servants and scribes; all of them men.

Paper was made from the Papyrus plant. It grew along the Nile banks and was pulped and rolled then dried.

See:

Hieroglyphs Pg 23
Scribes Pg 25
Education Pg 27

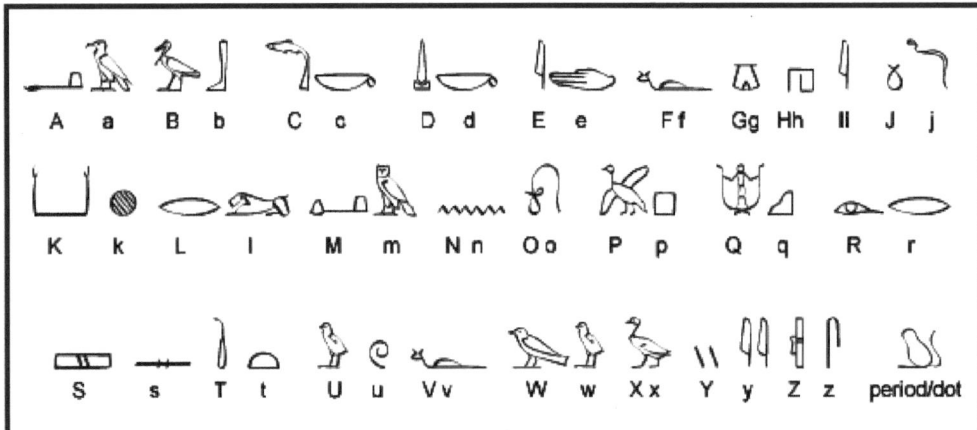

Hieroglyphic Alphabet.

Hieroglyphs

The Greek word for sacred writing is hieroglyph, which is the ancient Egyptian writing system. It consists of images of objects, people or elements from everyday life, or symbols related to letters or words. The system used three types of symbols.

*Ideograms: symbols that represent a thing or concept: cow, sun, house, the action of working, dancing.

*Determinatives: These are placed after the symbols and have a purely distinguishing value. There are approximately 100 of them and they clarify the meaning of the preceding symbol. For example, after a name it would indicate male or female.
A falcon, for instance, would show that the name before belonged to a god. Determinatives cannot be pronounced.

*Phonograms: These are the hardest to understand, but basically they are what we would call a consonant. They could be used as single letters or double as in ch, Th. But they also used them in threes, which does not exist in our language.

RAMESSES

The cartouche of Ramesses II is shown above as an example.
The first round symbol represented the sun and was pronounced RA.
The second symbol means 'day of birth' and is pronounced MICE. It therefore stands for M. The third and forth symbol is the letter S. Because there are no vowels they all become phonograms and are pronounced meSeS. RA +MESS+ES or 'RA created him'.
See section on Pharaohs page 65 for Cartouche explanation.

The Rosetta Stone

In 1799 in the village of Rosetta, a young officer in the Napoleon army found a strange black stone while doing some excavation work. His name was Pierre-Francois Bouchard, and being well educated he knew the stone must be important. It was taken to the scholars of Alexandria, but fell into the hands of the British when Nelson defeated the French in the Nile. It now stands in the British Museum.

The three different texts on the stone are Hieroglyphs, Demotic script and Greek. The Frenchman, Jean-Francois Champollion deciphered the stone.

Although the Rosetta stone is incomplete, it is still a sizeable monument, 45in in height and weighing 762Kgs.

The inscription on the stone is a decree - issued by the priests of Memphis in 196BC. It is in honour of Ptolemy V, and states how the Pharaoh served Egypt well in his eight-year reign.

Jean-Franois Champollion devoted his life to the study of Ancient Egypt and its writing system. Around 1817 he worked on the Rosetta stone and published his work in 1822. However, it was not the stone that provided the key to the mystery of hieroglyphs. Although he had compiled work of his study on the Greek and Demotic script on the stone, it was as he studied the cartouche of Ramesses II that he realised hieroglyphs could represent object and sound. He spent the last years of his life visiting Egypt but spent most of his time confined to bed with ill health. He died in 1832 at the age of 42.

Scribes

Although in the Middle Kingdom schools called the House of Life were used for the teaching of this profession, the skills of a scribe were usually passed down from father to son. Training would begin at the age of 5 and continue to the age of 12. In later life when very experienced, the scribe would become a very important and high-ranking official in the services of the Pharaoh.

Left: Seated scribe statue.
As an important official in the Egyptian State he would have many duties, including recording the annual floods and the boundaries of pastures, the harvest yield for tax assessment and keeping accounts of live stock and food in the royal warehouse. He would also be called upon to record legal judgements and contracts.
The scribes had their own protecting God, Thoth. Shown as a baboon or often as the Ibis headed God, Thoth was the inventor of writing and the calendar.

Writing materials and Papyrus

The scribe would always carry his tools with him, even on a battlefield to count the number of dead. The writing materials were stored in a wicker box, which could be used as a writing support. The scribe would sit cross-legged on the floor with the box in front of him.

Right: Scribe's pallet. British Museum.
The pallet would have a slot in the middle for the reed pens and two indents (top) for the two colours of black and red. A small double pot would contain water to dilute his inks (pigments), one for each colour. Scribes that painted more detailed documents, such as the book of the dead, would have four extra indents for blue, yellow, white and green.

Left: This sign for scribes shows three elements of their tools.
The pallet left, Inkwells right and in the middle a drawstring bladder for carrying water.
This is also the hieroglyph that means 'to write'.

Papyrus

The Ancient Egyptians would write on nearly any surface that would take ink or carving. The carvings on the walls of temples and tombs can still be seen, but it is also likely that the early Egyptians used materials such as palm leaves for notes and documents, and these did not survive.

The Papyrus grows in abundance in the swampy areas of the Nile. It was the sign of Lower Egypt and was often shown entwined with the Lotus plant of Upper Egypt to depict a united Egypt. But they also had many uses for the plant.

The lower part could be eaten as a vegetable, with the fibrous bark being used to make rope, baskets and sandals. Although an expensive process they also used it to make writing surfaces and became the inventors of paper.

The stem would be cut into strips roughly the same length and thickness. The first layer of strips were laid alongside each other and the second layer over the top of the first at right angles. *(Drawing below)* Both layers were moistened and beaten so the fibres would join together to form one single sheet with a furry texture. Once dry a flat stone was used to polish the surface. In the 1st millennium AD, papyrus was replaced by parchment and then paper. Today tourists can buy papyrus painted with ancient pictures *(left)*. This picture hangs in the house of the author. The edges of the picture clearly show the strips roughly cut and the crossed layers can still be seen.

Papyrus was always kept for the most important documents. The word papyrus comes from the Egyptian phrase, 'pa-en-per-ac', and meaning 'Belonging to the Pharaoh'.
This alone showed the importance of the papyrus paper.

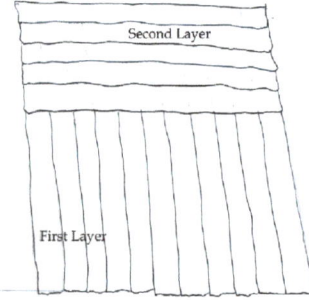

Education

With the age-old ways of farming and crafts such as carpentry being passed down from father to son, Egyptian schools were provided for the more privileged. These would be attended by the sons of civil servants such as scribes and other high dignitaries. Sometimes boys of a lower standard were allowed into the school if there was a growing need for civil servants and this gave them a rare opportunity to move up in society. However, education was basically for the children of the rich and powerful.

Boys would begin school at the age of five and start by learning to read and write in the most common everyday style. All would be taught Calculations, Geography and Science. Later, those chosen for priests and artists would learn hieroglyphs and sacred writing. Physical education such as swimming, exercise and even controlled fighting was encouraged. Something very important to all levels of Egyptian society was moral value. All children were taught to respect their parents and superiors, but inferiors were to be treated correctly and not humiliated by higher ranks.

Some old text even records the use of a cane as punishment for bad behaviour or laziness.

Other than a servant or midwife, few professions were open to girls. In all social levels including the rich, young girls were raised at home by their mothers. They would be taught cooking, weaving and general household jobs. The girls of the rich would learn dancing and acrobatics and for fun could play with their wooden or clay dolls.

There is little known about the training of a future pharaoh, but the Prince would attend a special school. Physical and military training was a higher priority than academic education. The future King was being prepared for leading his armies and the people.

Left: Wooden image of young boy at his desk.
Early in the first Dynasty the Egyptians realised the need for education.
It was important in the organisation and management of the country. They set up the world's first education system.

Chapter 4

Page 29. Everyday life.
Brewing & farming.
Page 30. Medicine.
Page 31. Clothing
Perfume & cosmetics.
Page 32. Hygiene.
Page 33. Toys & Games. Pets
Page 34. Counting

Everyday life

Brewing beer

The ancient Egyptians brewed beer as a part of a stable diet and also as offerings to the deceased to drink in the afterlife. Many tomb paintings and statues show the process of brewing.
Beer cakes where made using wheat and barley, these were lightly cooked and then crumbled into a sieve and water was added. The liquid was placed in heated jars and yeast was added for fermentation and dates for the sugar.
The fermentation of every day beer was short and produced low alcohol strength, but during festivals and the supply to royalty stronger beer was made and flavoured with honey and herbs.

Farming

The most important part of farming was the flooding of the Nile.
Farmers would first irrigate the fields before planting crops. Oxen were used to plough the fields and the main crops were wheat for bread and beer, and flax for clothing (*see linen*) and linseed oil. Other crops consisted mostly of beans, peas, garlic, onions, radish, cabbage and lettuce.
All harvest yields were recorded by the King's scribe. This was because all land belonged to the Pharaoh or priests; farmers were just labour.
Live stock consisted of cattle, goats, sheep, pigs, donkeys and pigeons. Crops and harvest was an important part of the economy, so a great majority of the population worked as farmers.

Farmers cutting corn. Tomb of Mennah.

Medicine

Medicine was practised from the very early years by the Egyptians and even the Greeks and Romans centuries after admired their skills.

Doctors were assisted by nurses who would also be skilled in massage and wound dressing. The doctors would not only look after the sick, but carried out beauty treatment, veterinary surgery and even pest control such as flies, insects and rats.

They worshiped Toth, God of wisdom and Sekhmet, the Goddess who took pity on human suffering and who was believed to the inventor of medicine.

Most medicine derived from plants but minerals and animal products were used. One common complaint was eye problems, caused by sunlight, wind and sands. This was treated with Ox liver and was quite successful. Liver extract is still used today for eye cures as it is associated with vitamin deficiency and contains vitamin A.

Bees were kept for their honey, not only to be used in brewing and eating but honey also had anti bacterial properties.

There are medical records for treatment on men, including fertility and prevention of conception. The first aim of Ancient Egyptian women was to produce heirs. However, very little is known about pregnancy and childbirth around this time.

It is believed that the death rate of baby and mother was high and medicine gave way to magic and help from Gods and Goddesses.

The wall carving above shows medicine in numerous jars, medical instruments
And even 2 mothers sitting upon birthing stalls (left).
Kom Ombo temple

Clothing

As mentioned previously in farming, flax was a major crop and was used to make linen and linseed oil. Fragments of clothes dating back to 4400 BC have been found in excavations. The plant was harvested by hand and the oil removed. The stems were beaten and the fibres combed to strengthen them. The strands would then be spliced together and spun on a spindle. Young Flax would make a delicate thread while older would create a stronger fibre used in matting. Most ancient Egyptian clothing was white but colour became fashionable during the 18th Dynasty.

Early clothing was basic, consisting of a triangle fabric covering the waist and knees, known as a loincloth and held in place by a fabric or leather belt.

The only thing that distinguished class was jewellery. It was not until during the new kingdom that clothing became elegant. Skirts were worn short or ankle length and short sleeved tunics were worn.

Perfume & Cosmetics

Although originally used only for religious ceremonies, perfume became a part of everyday life for Ancient Egyptians from the earliest times. Priests would use scented oils and extracts of flowers to please the Gods. There are many wall paintings of Pharaohs making offerings of fragrances to Gods.

Priests realised that they could make money from the sale of perfumes but they were expensive and only the rich could afford them.

Ancient Egyptians focused on making the eyes look larger and wanted to emphasize shape. Ground green Malachite was mixed with water to make a paste and applied around the eyelids. In later periods black Kohl from the mineral Galena was used as it had therapeutic value, protecting the eyes from the sun, sands and flies.

Left: The statue shows a Pharaoh wearing a skirt like garment known as a Shendyt. This would also be worn by soldiers and workers, probably for ease of movement, but the Pharaohs' would have been of the finest materials.
Right: Malachite, a copper carbonate hydroxide mineral used in green paint until the 1800s.

Hygiene

Perhaps due to the heat, the Egyptians spent a lot of time removing dirt from themselves and life around them. The numerous toilet items excavated tell us of the importance of cleanliness. In many palaces and homes of important people archaeologists have discovered washrooms. Lower classes would wash outside with bowls of water.

Oils were used to scent and protect the skin and berries or honey used to sweeten the breath.

The Egyptian women took great care of their hair, treating it with oils and combing with ivory combs. They would wear wigs made of real hair for the wealthy and wool for the poor. Most men had shaven heads. It was practical but wigs could be worn by men as a status symbol. Beards were only grown if there was a death in the family as a sign of mourning. *(See page 78: The beard of Osiris)*

The Pharaoh was a living God and would always appear in all his splendour. He would be washed several times a day, receive a pedicure and manicure and be shaved of all bodily hair. He would wear a false curved beard of the Gods, the only time he wore a straight one was when he represented Ptah, the creator God. For everyday duties he would normally wear the Nemes headdress, a striped cloth pulled across the forehead and tied at the back. If he wore the royal crown the front would be adorned with a rearing cobra called Uraeus and the vulture Nekhbet.

Nekhbet, the Goddess of Upper Egypt, protects the king with her wings. Uraeus represented the Goddess Wadjet of Lower Egypt, and shows the kings power over life and death.

Left: The cobra and vulture on the golden death mask of Tutankhamen.
Right: The lid of a canopic jar shows the Pharaoh wearing the striped Nemes headdress.

Toys & Games

Children were encouraged to play with toys and games as an instructive part of life. Wall paintings depict boys in battle games to enhance their skills and strength. Girls would play ball games or could often be found dancing.

Wooden and clay figures of dolls have been found and wooden lions, crocodiles and other animals on a base with wheels for pulling along.
The most popular adult game was Senet, played on a board of squares or even scratched on to the ground. This was very similar to chess or draughts.

Left: This fine example of a Senet board was found in the tomb of Tutankhamun, Placed there for the King in the afterlife.

Pets

Bastet

Cats and dogs are often found mummified in the tombs of their owners. Cats were the most common household pet. There were two main types, the jungle cat and the African wild. From the Middle Kingdom they are often shown on tomb walls as part of the family. It is believed that early Egyptian farmers domesticated cats to keep down vermin in the grain stores.

The cat soon became depicted as the daughter of the sun God, Ra and a gentle protective Goddess. Bastet was seen as protector of the Pharaoh and guardian of the two lands, Lower and Upper Egypt. The cats were highly respected and it was forbidden for anyone to harm them. However, this did not apply to ritual killings carried out by priests and there are many animal cemeteries with mummified cats and other animals. L*eft: The two figures of Bastet, (author's house) show the normal representation of many bronze statues found. Some would have gold rings in their ears and nose. A Temple was erected for her in the Delta city of Bubastis.*

Counting & Measuring

What we know about numbers and measuring systems in Ancient Egypt comes from leather and papyrus scrolls and wooden tablets. They show the four basic calculations of addition, subtraction, multiplication and division. They were able to calculate the area of triangles and circles, as well as volumes of cylinders and of course, pyramids.

Numbers were carved or written as figures instead of words.
The picture above shows the dates of religious festivals recorded on the wall at the temple of Kom Ombo. A single vertical line represented 1 and each other symbol represented multiples of 10, 100, 1000 and so on.

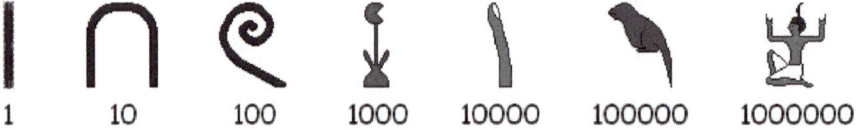

The above pictures show the signs for each number.

The signs above show how the characters were used, this figure would total to 113.

Chapter 5
Cities & Temples along the Nile

Page 36. Heliopolis
Page 37. Abu Simbel
Page 38. Abu Simbel, The Relocation.
Page 39. Abu Simbel, The Sun Rays.
Page 40. Alexandria.
Page 41. Akhetaten, Tell el-armarna
Page 42. Karnak
Page 43. Karnak Continued.
Page 44. Luxor (Theabes)
Page 45. Luxor Continued.
Page 46. Edfu
Page 47. Memphis
Page 48. Philae
Page 49. Cairo
Page 50. Dier el-bahari
Page 51. Kom Ombo
Page 52. Obelisks (The unfinished)
Page 53. Giza (Pyramids)
Page 54. Pyramid Construction.
Page 55. Burial sites
Page 56. Artisans & Labourers
Page 57. The Sphinx
Page 58. Valley of the Kings
Page 59. Valley of the Queens
Page 60. Tomb construction.

Heliopolis

City of the Sun

Although the origins of the City of the Sun are not known, its religious importance dates back to 5000-3000BC, before the dynasty period. Heliopolis started to evolve as the spiritual capital of a united Egypt and the first sun temple was built there in the early New Kingdom.

The priests of the city believed in a divine dynasty of nine Gods, the main one being the sun God Atum in his many forms. From Atum arose Shu-air, and Tefnut-water, who produced Geb-earth, and Nut-sky. The union of Geb and Nut resulted in the birth of Osiris, Isis, Seth and Nepthys.

At the start of the Old Kingdom the priests divided the sun God into groups of Gods. Atum, as Khepri, became the God of morning, who rose with the sun on his back. Atum, as Ra, the midday sun and Atum as the sunset. By the 5th Dynasty Heliopolis was the cult centre for the sun God RA. The city was now so important to the Pharaoh that they built copies of it all over Egypt.

All that remains of the city today is an excavated mud brick wall, 1100m long and 475 wide, which surrounded the site. This is believed to be from the New Kingdom, 18-20th dynasty, but a plan of the temple inscribed on a sheet of stone shows a temple built by Senusret 1 in the 12th Dynasty. He erected two obelisks of pink granite, each 20m high and weighing 20 tonnes. Only one now stands in Northwest Cairo. Another two obelisks erected by Tuthmosis III of the 18th dynasty are now in New York and London. They are known as Cleopatra's needle.

The best evidence of how the city may have looked comes from the Solar Temple built at Abu Gurab, a copy of Heliopolis built in the 5th Dynasty by Nyuserra (2445-2414.)
In the time of Ramesses II the temple of Heliopolis had more than 12000 people in its service. However the city was abandoned after Alexandria became the main centre of Egypt. Heliopolis means, City of Sun, and was the main place of worship for the sun god, Ra.
Left: The obelisk known as Cleaopatras needle is actually the obelisk of Tuthmosis III and stands on the bank of the river Thames in London. Damage from bombs dropped in the 2nd World War can be seen all around its surface.
Old Kingdom 2686-2181Bc. New Kingdom 1570-1070 Bc.

Abu Simbel

The temple of Abu Simbel, almost on the borders of Sudan, still defies the centuries. It was one of the most imposing constructions built by one of the greatest Egyptian Pharaohs, Ramesses II. Under the reign of Ramesses the boarders of Egypt stretched to Syria and Nubia. Abu Simbel was built and stood as a symbol of his divine power to all. Under and between his feet are the figures that represent his enemies.

Left: The author and his partner stand in front of the awesome temple of Abu Simbel. Carved directly into the rock, the front consists of 4 colossal statues of Ramesses. Inside, the walls are decorated with stories of his military glory over the Hittites in the 5th year of his reign. The paintings were well preserved by the huge amount of sands blown through the entrance over the years.

Discovered in 1813 by Jean-Louis Burckhadt, almost completely hidden beneath the sands, the temple was not excavated until 7 years later by Giovanni Belzoni.

Right: The smaller temple at Abu Simbel was dedicated to his wife, Nefertari. The entrance has 6 10 metre high statues, 4 of the King and 2 of his wife. The Queen wears the crown with the cow horns and the sun disc of the Goddess Hathor. Unusually for its time, the Queen is shown the same height as the Pharaoh; perhaps a sign of his love for Nefertari.
Nefertari was the wife of Ramesses II and should not be confused with Nefertiti, wife of Akhenaten and believed mother of Tutankhamun.

The Relocation of Abu Simbel

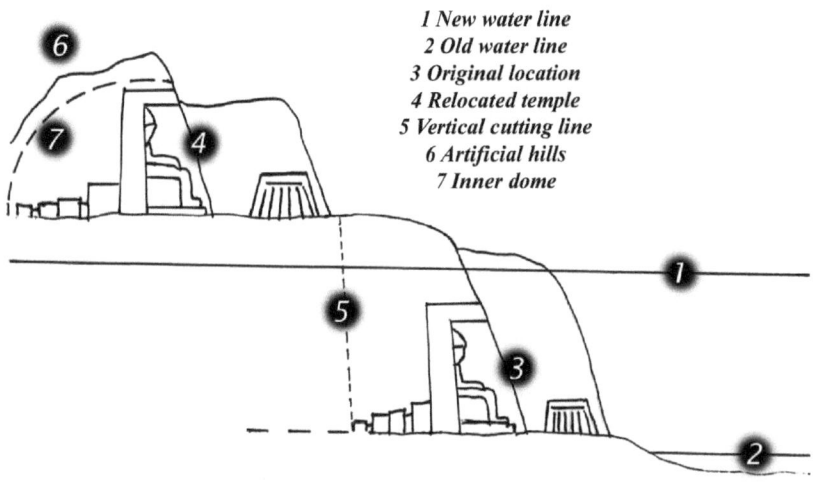

1 New water line
2 Old water line
3 Original location
4 Relocated temple
5 Vertical cutting line
6 Artificial hills
7 Inner dome

The building of the second and highest Aswan dam threatened to engulf the temple of Abu Simbel under water. In 1960 the Egyptian minister of culture appealed for world-wide help to relocate villagers and rescue any temple or monument that would be lost. Finally, with financial help from 50 countries, the largest archaeological salvage took place between 1960 and 1965. Some of the smaller temples were given to Italy, Spain, The Netherlands and United States in recognition for their help.

The temple of Abu Simbel was relocated 64 metres higher than its original location and 180 metres inland. Both temples were built of sandstone blocks, the largest temple weighing a total of 15,000 tonnes and the smaller temple of Nefertari 3,500 tonnes.

The temples were cut into 1,036 numbered blocks, some weighing 30 tonnes, and moved to its new location against a false mountain, The mountain is actually hollow with a large dome inside which houses the temple's inner shrine.

The temple was positioned so that the rays of the sun would penetrate down the great entrance hall and hit the back wall of the sanctuary, illuminating three of the four seated Gods (*Above*). The fourth god was Ptah who was connected with the underworld and so was always in darkness.

This would occur every year on the 22nd October and the 22nd February. It is believed the dates correspond with the King's birthday and coronation but there is no evidence to support this. For whatever reason, this was an amazing feat of construction for nearly 3300 years ago.

Because of the relocation of the temple and the drift of the tropic of cancer these dates have changed by one day now occurring on the 21st of October and February.

Left: The ceiling of the entrance is painted with images of the vulture goddess Nekhbet. She was the protector of the King. The rows of statues along the left wall show the Pharaoh wearing the crown of Upper and Lower Egypt.

(The tropic of cancer, also called the Northern tropic, is a circle of latitude on the earth that marks the most northerly position that the sun may appear directly overhead).

Alexandria

Alexandria is the second largest City in Egypt, built by Alexander the Great. He realised the lack of important outlets on the Mediterranean and gave orders to his architect Dinocrates to begin planning. However, Alexander himself did not spend much time in the city during his life, and it was under his successors, the Ptolemis, that Alexandria became the capital. In 48 BC during the reign of Cleopatra, the city was laid siege by Caesar and became a Roman province.

In the 15th century the Turkish Sultan Qaitbaty had a massive fortress built beside the harbour. Up to 1326 this was the site of the Lighthouse of Alexandria, the earliest known lighthouse and one of the Seven Wonders of the World. It collapsed after several earthquakes. Built in the reign of Ptolemy II, it stood 135 metres high and had a fire burning night and day inside the top.

Alexander the Great

Born in 356BC, he was taught by Aristotle and became King at the age of 23. Regarded as the greatest general of all time, he set out to conquer Asia. Within 10 years he had an Empire stretching from Macedonia to Egypt, Afghanistan to India. When he died of malaria aged 33, his empire was divided between his Generals. Egypt fell to the Ptolemy dynasty.

Left: Bust of Alexander the great. The location of his Tomb is still a mystery.

Right: Bust of Roman emperor Julius Caesar.

Akhetaten

Tell el-amarna

Akhetaten was the capital of Egypt during the reign of the "heretic" Pharaoh, Amenhotep IV. (*Later he renamed himself Akhenatan*)
The aerial picture above shows the remains of houses covered by centuries of sands, all that is left of a city which spanned 21sq miles along the Nile. It was situated on the East bank about 194 miles south of modern Cairo. Much that is known about the city comes from preserved boundary stelae* ringing the perimeter of the remains. There are13 in all, cut into the cliffs both sides of the Nile.
This once splendid city of the schismatic* king disappeared with the death of its creator.

To understand more of this city, please see Pharaohs, chapters on Amenhotep IV.
Heretic: Someone who has a belief very different to an established custom.

* Schismatic/Schism; The division of a religion/group.
* Stelae is a stone or wooden slab used to publish laws and decrees or as boundary markers.

Karnak
The Temple of Amun

The temple of Karnak contains three precincts surrounded by an enclosure wall. They are dedicated to Amun, his wife Mut and the God of war, Montu.
The biggest precinct, the only one accessible to the public, is that of Amun. With its succession of pylons, courts and columned halls, obelisks and sacred lake, it is the largest temple in the world.
The most overwhelming site in the precinct of Amun is the great Hypostyle hall. Built by Seti I and his son Ramesses II, it contains 134 columns. The middle row consists of a processional avenue of 14 columns, 23 metres high and 15 metres around the base.

Right: The 14 columns of the processional avenue. The nearest pillars show the results of repairs, but further into the row the middle columns are better preserved.

Below: The underside of the lintels across the columns in the Hypostyle hall still shows the well preserved colours of the reliefs.

Below Right: Some of the 134 columns of the great Hypostyle hall covering 6000 square metres, large enough to hold St Peters Cathedral in Rome and St Pauls Cathedral London.
Some of the carvings show the Pharaohs making offerings to Amun. Others show the God Thoth inscribing the story of Seti I's reign.

Work began on the temple around the 12th dynasty, but most of what can be seen today dates from the New Kingdom, a time of wealthy and powerful Pharaohs. Almost all rulers of this period extended and redecorated some parts of the temple.

Top left: Obelisks of Hatshepsut *(front)* and her father Tuthmosis I behind.

Top Right: Statue of Amun.

Left: The exterior of the west wall on the 7th pylon shows scenes of Ramesses II battle against Syrians and the peace with the Hittites in the 21st year of his reign.

Below: Boat shrine of Sety II.
Left: One of the huge pylons at Karnak. A pylon was a monumental gateway, usually consisting of 2 tapering towers.

Luxor
Thebes

Luxor temple, known to the Ancient Egyptians as Thebes, was built mainly by two Pharaohs, Amenhotep III and Ramesses II. Work was approved under the reign of Akhenaten, the son of Amenhotep III, but it resumed under Tutankhamun and Horemheb.
The temple of Luxor however, reached its height of glory under Ramesses II.

The two seated figures in front of the pylon are Ramesses II. The missing obelisk now stands on the Place de la Concorde in France. Note the four large niches cut into the pylon used to hold giant flagpoles.
The main purpose of the temple was the annual festival of Opet. The statue of Amun, Mut and Khons would be taken from their sanctuaries at Karnak in ceremonial barges to Luxor. During the night, the rebirth of Amun took place and this would symbolise the renewal of the world. The festival was held at the end of the Nile's annual floods. Therefore, the plants growing in the fields shortly after were signs of new life.

Amun

Although worshipped from as early as the 11th Dynasty, it was around the time of the New Kingdom (*18th Dynasty*) that Amun was considered the greatest of all Egyptian gods. His cult now centred at Karnak in the largest and richest temple in the land.
Amun was combined with several other Gods, the most significant was the powerful Sun god Ra, to become Amun-Ra.

Right: Statue of the God Amun and his consort, the Goddess Mut.

Top left: One of the colossal statues of Ramesses II, which stand between the columns in the courtyard of the temple.

Top right: The author stands in front of a seated figure of Ramesses II at the entrance to the colonnade of Amenhotep III. The weathered figure of Nefertari, the Pharaoh's wife, can just be seen standing to the left of the king's leg.

Above left: The cartouche of Ramesses II found carved on the side of both seated figures that stand each side of the entrance pylon. The clarity of the carving is due to the temple being covered over for many years in desert sands.

Above right: Hundreds of human headed sphinxes were placed along the processional way between Karnak and Luxor during the reign of Nectanebo I.

Edfu

The best-preserved temple in Egypt, dedicated to the falcon headed God Horus, stands in what is now the town of Edfu. This is where the statue of Horus wearing the double crown of Upper and Lower Egypt can be seen. Tuthmosis III started the temple, but the newer temple was started by Ptolemy III in 237BC and continued up to Cleopatra, the last Queen of Egypt.

During ancient times a statue of Horus would be carried to the rooftop so the God could be revitalised by the sun. After, he would be returned to the middle sanctuary where offerings would be made. This ritual is shown around the walls of the temple.

Horus wears the double crown, temple of Edfu. This is one statue that I looked forward to seeing when I visited the temple in 2001.

Memphis

Very little remains of the ancient Memphis, which extended for 15 km. Believed to have been built by the great architect Imhotep. It contained a wealth of temples and sanctuaries dedicated to gods. During the New Kingdom, Thebes became the main Egyptian City. But Memphis served as the capital of the North. The decline began with the creation of Alexandria. Today only a few ruins remain. The most important of these is the temple of Ptah, where all Pharaohs were crowned.

Below: Part of the Ptah temple complex at Memphis.

Ptah was the creator God of Memphis, God of craftsmen and architects.
Memphis comes from the word Men-nefer, meaning 'established and beautiful'.

Above: This magnificent statue of Ramesses II once stood 13.5 metres high outside Cairo train station. It now lays on display at Mit Rahina, old Memphis.

Philae

The temple of Philae stands on an island in the middle of the Nile and is dedicated to the Goddess Isis. When the first dam was built the temple was completely submerged by the new water level. With the building of the new dam the temple would have been lost forever. In between 1972 and 1980 the temple was relocated to the nearby island of Aglika, which was landscaped to look like the original island.

Above: Approaching the temple by boat.

On its original grounds, Philae stood opposite the island of Biga. The Ancient Egyptians believed this to be the burial site of the God Osiris, husband of Isis. Biga was forbidden to all but the priesthood. Therefore all public festivals were held on the island of Philae.

Left: The relief on the right pylon shows the Pharaoh making offerings to Horus and Hathor. Hathor is seen in many reliefs as she was associated with Isis. The large stone beneath the feet was erected by Ptolemy and tells of gifts of land to the temple.
Below: The Pharaoh is seen killing his enemies on the left pylon

Cairo

Old and New

Present-day Cairo can be traced back to the Egyptian capital of Memphis. Although the Pharaohs moved their cities up and down the Nile a capital always remained in the north because of the strategic location for the Mediterranean. After being conquered by the Arabs in 639 the city was given the name, Al-qauira (*Cairo*) meaning the victorious. Cairo, the largest city in the African and Arab world and capital of Egypt, has an overcrowded population of 7 million. The urban development is running out of control, with housing blocks springing up at alarming rates. The city is a mixture of cultures, with three religions existing together. Muslims, Jews and Christian-Coptic. (Christian community of 5th- 8th century Egypt)

Left: Egyptian Museum, Cairo. Founded in 1858 by Auguste Mariette, one of the pioneers of Egyptology. It has the finest collection of Egyptian works, including the magnificent treasures of Tutankhamun.

Below.
Cairo is a city choked with traffic. From the narrow streets to the expressways. With the noise of horns, the shouts of vendors, newspaper sellers and shoe shiners and the summoning of the faithful to prayer.

Dier-el Bahari

One of the most magnificent sites at the Valley of the Kings (see page 58), is the mortuary temple of Queen Hatshepsut. Built largely of sandstone, it rose in three terraces to a central sanctuary. The lower chamber to the right of the steps shows reliefs of Hatshepsut's birth. The left chamber shows the story of her journeys to Punt where she traded for living trees and plants to place outside the temple.

Above: The author and partner standing in front of the temple. The cliff that the temple was cut into can be seen. In ancient times the foreground would have been covered in trees and fountains. The remains of a few 3500 year old trees still remain.

Above Left: The relief shows the vivid colours still seen on the walls, in this case the vulture.
Above right: Statues of Hatshepsut line the upper terrace. Unfortunately after her death, her bitter son Tuthmosis III had many of her reliefs destroyed.

Kom Ombo

The Temple of Haroeris and Sobek

In ancient times Kom Ombo was a stop off point for traders into Nubia and roads to the gold mines. Unlike others in the valley, the temple still stands beside the bank of the Nile. Although sands from the desert covered most of the temple for years, the Nile washed away the front pylon and forecourt long ago. The two inner sanctuaries were dedicated to Haroeris, the older form of Horus and Sobek, the crocodile god.

Approaching the temple from the Nile. A beautiful site to be seen at night when the temple is lit up.

The pictures above of a roof lintel and right of a pillar, show the colours that were preserved by the sands despite time.

The Obelisk

The first stone to resemble the obelisk was in the Temple of the Sun God at Helliopolis and was placed where the Ancient Egyptians believed the first rays of the sun hit the earth. The obelisk then developed into a tall pointed pillar, carved from one piece of stone. The tip would be covered in gold to catch the first and last rays of the day. The oldest existing obelisk is that of Senusret I and was erected in the Middle Kingdom.
By the New Kingdom they were more widely used and normally stood as a pair in the front of a temple. The four sides would be inscribed with the King's title and praise to the sun God, RA.

The top picture shows the remaining tip from the broken obelisk of Hatshepsut at the temple of Karnak.

The unfinished obelisk
Right:
In granite quarry near Aswan lies the unfinished obelisk. If completed it would have stood 42 metres high and weighed 1160 tons. It is believed this obelisk would have been one of a pair standing before the temple of Tuthmosis III at Karnak.
The first obelisk to stand at this site is now in Rome and is the largest in the World.

Giza & The Great Pyramids

Giza, on the West Bank of the Nile, is the site of one of the seven wonders of the Ancient World, the only one still standing; the great pyramid of Khufu. Wanting to break with the tradition of stepped pyramids, the Pharaoh Khufu believed that the smooth sides would make it easier for the soul to ascend to heaven. The sun represented a cosmic union, which would pass via the top of the pyramid, down the walls and into the ground. The tomb was seen as a link between earthly life and the hereafter.

Three pyramids were built at Giza. Khufu built the 1st and biggest, his son Khafre built the 2nd and grandson Menkaure the 3rd.
They lie in such a way that neither will hide the other from the sun at any time. Although Khufu's looks smaller than his sons, it stands on a lower area of ground and is actually bigger.

Construction

Two types of blocks were used in the construction; hard Granite for the main bulk of the building and softer sandstone for the finishing and smooth sides. As the picture above shows, the sandstone was removed by locals years later and used in nearby buildings. The cap on the top of Khafre's pyramid is the remains of this sandstone.

The hard granite came from quarries 800km away in Aswan. The sandstone was found nearby. Fires were started on the ground and then put out with water. The temperature change would cause cracks in the stone into which wood wedges were placed. These would then be soaked with water and expanded, splitting the rock. The base was severed from the ground by mallet and chisel. It was then shaped into a square before being moved to the site. Attempts have been made over hundreds of years to find the answer to how the pyramids were built. The great pyramid itself took 20 years to construct, and the height at which the blocks are placed is an amazing feat.

The most commonly accepted theory is that ramps spiralled around the pyramid as it was built *(p54)*. These were removed after the last stone was placed on top. This stone would have been coated in Gold or Silver to reflect the rays of the sun.

Cont:

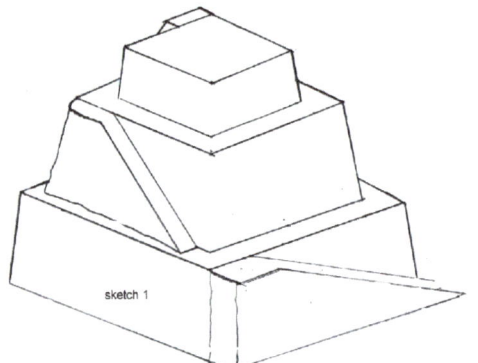

sketch 1

It is believed the blocks were placed on wooden sledges and pulled up the slopes with ropes by teams of men. Water was tipped ahead of the sledge to lubricate the ground.
The ramps were made of mud mixed with limestone. As the basic structure was erected, craftsman added the white limestone that gave the pyramid its smooth and shiny exterior. The ramps were then demolished.

The workforce

It is estimated that the blocks would have been put in place at a rate of one every 5 minutes. This would of course take a huge workforce, and it is believed that hordes of slaves tied to endless ropes were used. As this was a period when Egypt was more concerned with internal affairs, there were no prisoners of war or slaves as popularly maintained.
This was also proven in 1990 when the tomb of a worker was discovered near to the pyramids. Within months of the discovery, 250 graves were uncovered, an entire cemetery for workers.
Hieroglyphics on the entrance to tombs showed the builders to be highly regarded craftsman. They also gave evidence to job titles such as Foreman, Director of Buildings and even Inspector of Buildings.
On the same site a bakery was excavated, even the means for brewing beer were discovered. The bones of workmen with injuries such as breaks or crushing showed signs of good medical treatment.
These were not badly treated slaves, but craftsmen with families and though the work was hard, there is evidence of workmen having free time and even holidays.

Left: Although not at the pyramid site but actually rising against the first pylon at Karnak, this picture shows a part of a ramp built entirely from mud bricks. The same type would have been used in the building of pylons, temples and pyramids.

Burial sites

Tombs and Pyramids

Early tombs were known as Mastabas. They were rectangle in plan, with slightly sloping sides. Later this type was used beside or near the pyramid for the burial of the pharaoh's nobles, officials and even craftsman.

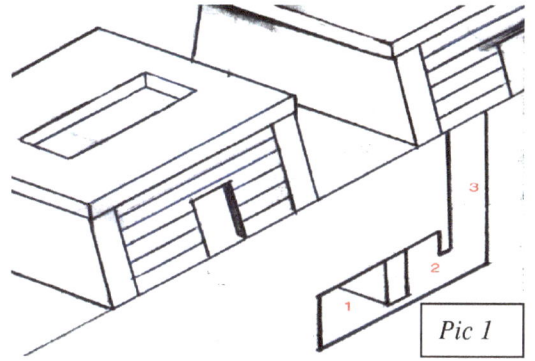

Pic 1
1 Burial chamber
2 Gifts and belongings
3 Shaft

Pic 1

Pharaohs then began to have pyramids built. They believed that by being entombed in such an eternal resting place, they could protect their kingdom forever. The pyramid did not mark the end of existence, but the beginning of eternal life. Also, the pharaoh was now the most important person in Egypt. There was no need for him to wander the land like his predecessors. Now he could build a city, usually with his burial site near by.

The pharaoh Djoser (see page 68) had his royal architect, Imhotep, build the first pyramid. This is known as the step pyramid and stands at Saqqara, the oldest and largest cemetery in Egypt, situated 30 km from Cairo.

Above. The bottom layer of the step pyramid was basically a large mastaba, and the next four steps were placed on top. It stands 62m high with a base of 125x109m. An extraordinary number of rooms, tunnels and galleries were found under the pyramid.

Artisans And Labourers

Contrary to belief, the pyramids, tombs and temples of Egypt were not built by slaves but ordinary artisans and labourers. Approximately a mile south of the Kings' valley is the excavated site that was once the village of Deir el-Medina. Here we can see the remains of houses where workman lived with their families.

During their ten-day shift they would stay near the tombs in huts, then return home on their rest days. Some would use their days off to make paintings, carvings and furniture for private clients.

One of the most important and interesting finds at the site was thousands of limestone fragments called Ostraca. These inscribed stones were used to keep records and tell us the names of residents, where they lived and when they died. We can even tell if they were taken ill, went on holiday and what they ate, bought and sold.

Ostraca
Pieces of limestone used to record all sorts of daily life, such as wages for workers. Many craftsmen and their families were buried in tombs of their own. The information from these stones does not show a workforce of slaves.

The bulk of the workforce came from peasantry. In the months of the Nile floods all labour was put on the Pharaoh's latest project. When a major structure such as the Great Pyramids required a large workforce for long periods, labour would be brought in from hundreds of miles around.

A worker would not receive a wage but would be paid in necessities such as wheat, dried meat and fish, onions, pulse and beer. They would also receive free water, clothing and tools.

Tools
Egyptian workers used massive wooden mallets with flat or pointed copper or bronze chisels to carve and shape blocks. Lengths of string were used to mark out areas. The string could also be soaked in a red pigment then stretched across walls to mark out grids for paintings.

Artisan: Skilled workman or craftsman. See also sections on farming, beer and education.

The Sphinx

Guardian of Giza

The plateau of Giza is a vast necropolis *(graveyard)* of the Pharaoh Khufu, his offspring and their Queens. In front of the three great Pyramids stands the Sphinx, a huge statue in the shape of a lion, with a human head.

It was believed to have been built in the reign of Khafra *(son of Khufu)* and is said to represent him.

The word Sphinx is Greek, from the Egyptian word shepankh, which refers to the human headed lion that guards the underworld. The Sphinx is guards the necropolis. The body of the statue was slowly buried in the sands over thousands of years, and only the head was showing. The sands were removed in 1925 by the archaeologist Emile Baraize.

It is believed by some that there is a secret door at the base of the Sphinx between the feet, which may contain evidence of the lost city of Atlantis, or even the book of the dead. To date, the Egyptian authorities are reluctant to grant excavation.

Because of the soft limestone that the Sphinx is made of corrosion is extremely bad. Teams of restorers work on it constantly.

Left: Contrary to belief the Sphinx was not damaged by the Napoleon army. It is believed a 14th century sheikh ordered the smile to be wiped from its face.
The original head may have been replaced with the human head that is now seen, because it is so much smaller in the proportion to the body. But this is not known for sure.

Valley of the Kings

With the beginning of the New Kingdom (*18th Dynasty*) around 1550 BC, The new Kings based their capital in Upper Egypt at Thebes (now Luxor). This was a time of powerful and wealthy rulers and with tomb robbery now a serious problem, a new method of burial evolved.
The Pharaohs did not want to build monuments to show their final resting-places, but to hide their tombs away. It is not known for sure why this part of the Nile was chosen but some believe that the rulers of this period wanted to trace themselves back to their ancestors.
Thebes lay on the East bank with its great temples such as Karnak *(p42),* while on the West Bank a burial site was chosen and the tombs were cut into the rocks. The highest peak in the valley was naturally shaped like a pyramid and was known as el-Qurn. This resemblance may be another reason this site was chosen.

Right: On the approach to the Valley of the Kings stand two colossus statues known as the colossi of Memnon. The statues are carved in the image of a seated Amenhotep III, thought to be the founder of the valley.
Neither has fared well against weather and both have been rebuilt after falling over some years before. But standing 60ft high they are an impressive sight nevertheless.

Left: The valley itself is a dried up river bed of limestone and shale that has baked in the sun. But hidden within the tombs for thousands of years were some of the greatest artefacts ever found.
Rich colours can still be seen in the wall paintings and the sheer size of some tombs leaves visitors in wonder.
The natural shaped peak can be seen here.

Valley of the Queens

The ancient Egyptian name for the valley was Ta-set-neferu, meaning Place of the (royal) children. In the early eighteenth Dynasty the tombs were used for the burial of Princes, Princesses and people close to the royal family. The earliest burial of a Queen can be dated to the reign of Amenophis III. It was however not until the beginning of the nineteenth Dynasty that the site became the favoured burial place of Pharaohs wives. They also continued to use it for the royal children.

The valley contains around 75 tombs and most of them were discovered between 1903 to 1906 in an Italian expedition led by Ernesto Schiaparelli, curator of the Egyptian Museum in Turin. Included in these finds was the most important of decorated Queens' tombs, that of Nefertari, the favourite wife of Ramesses II.

Above: This wall from the tomb of Nefertari shows the gods welcoming the Queen into the afterlife. The sun God RA sits on both sides of the doorway. On the right he is the falcon headed god and on the left he has the head of the Scarab Khepri.

After years of cleaning to remove salt deposits the plasterwork has become very fragile. The salt deposits came from the water originally used in the plaster and paint, the valleys frequent flooding and even the sweat and breath of visitors in modern times. Restoration has been able to halt the process of decay but the only way to protect the tomb from the ravage of time is to restrict entrance to the public.

Tomb construction

Only a chosen few were meant to see the inside of the tomb when painted and filled with gifts and the deceased's belongings. They were not built to be a public memorial or to impress people. The tomb and its decoration were the beginning of a new life for the person enclosed.

A Pharaoh's tomb began the moment he took the throne of Egypt. This may be the reason why Tutankhamun's tomb is so small, because he died so young.

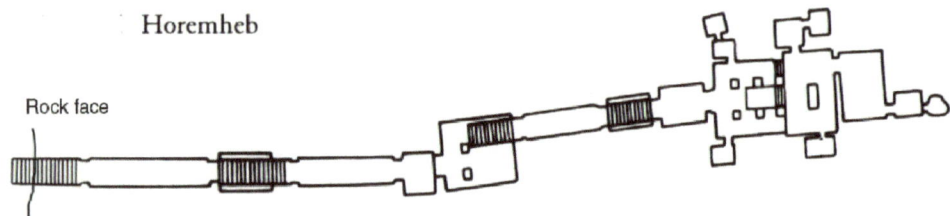

The layout above shows the tomb of Horemheb. Here we can see the depth of the tomb from the rock face and the many chambers. Compare this with the tomb of Tutankhamun. *(See Pharaohs-Tutankhamun p76)*

First the stone cutters chipped away at the rocks, carving out the hallways and chambers. Others followed and coated the rough walls with a plaster. Onto this artists would draw outlines of the tomb's subject. This could show the story of the deceased's life and even the journey to the afterlife. Sculptures would then carve out the pictures before a master painter finished them in beautiful colours. *(See section on Artisans and labourers p56)*

The ceilings were painted a deep blue colour and covered in stars. Then the sky goddess, NUT, would be painted arching and stretching across the sky from one end of the burial room to the other. The Egyptians believed that all heavenly bodies run their course through the body of NUT.

Right: This picture from the tomb of Ramesses VI shows Nut's head hanging down and her arms reaching to the floor.

Chapter 6

Pharaohs

Page 62. Intro
Page 63. The meaning of Pharaoh.
Page 64. A day in the life of the Pharaoh.
Page 65. Cartouches.
Page 66. The Pharaoh's Army.
Page 67. Narmer. Aha.
Page 68. Djoser. (Step Pyramid)
Page 69. Snefru
Page 70. The Great Pyramid builders. Khufu. Khafra. Menkaura.
Page 71. Userkaf. Pepi II
Page 72. Mentuhotep I
Page 73. The New Kingdom. Tuthmosis III
Page 74. Hatshepsut (Queen)
Page 75. Akhenaten.
Page 76. Tutankhamun.
Page 77. Treasures and Burial chamber of Tutankhamun.
Page 78. Items from tomb of Tutankhamun. Inc: Golden mask
Page 79. Horemheb.
Page 80. 19th Dynasty. Seti I
Page 81. Ramesses II.
Page 82. Ramesses II Continued.
Page 83. Ramesses II & Nefertari.
Page 84. Queen Twosret.
Page 85. 20th Dynasty.
Page 86, 87, 88, 89. The Pharaohs power weakens.
Page 90. Alexander the Great.
Page 91. Ptolemaic Period.
Page 92. Cleopatra.

Pharaohs

This section will cover the more important, better-known and most influential Pharaohs of each Dynasty. There will also be a mention of some Queens and offsprings.
The picture above is of Thutmose III, one of the greatest shapers of Egyptian history and a ruler that inspired fear in his enemies.

The Meaning of Pharaoh

Amun-Ra was the supreme creator of the universe, and the Pharaoh was seen as the earthly son of Amun-Ra. The Egyptians believed the first Pharaoh was the mythical God Horus, son of Osiris and Isis.

The human Pharaoh was considered to be the legitimate successor of Horus. He was the most sacred and powerful figure that protected his subjects and guaranteed their prosperity. As ruler he was responsible for keeping order in the world and opposing forces of chaos. Even the stars, Nile floods and human relations should be untroubled under his protection.

Because of the belief that any body of royal birth had heavenly blood flowing through their veins, it was not uncommon for related people such as brother and sister to marry. This they considered would preserve the purity of divine blood.

As the Pharaoh was often clean shaven, a false beard attached behind the ears was worn during festivals and was the symbol of immortality. In his hands he would hold the Heka (Sceptre) that symbolised the guiding of his people, and the Nekhakha (Whip) which showed his authority.

The Pharaoh had many crowns and head-dresses but for every day practical use he would wear the Nemes; a light cloth pulled back over the head. He would often wear a breast plate in the form of a vulture that resembled the Goddess of Upper Egypt, Nekhbet.

Left: The author's partner stands next to a statue thought to be Tuthmosis III, Karnak temple. Notice the Nemes head-dress pulled back over the head and draped down the shoulders.
Right: The statue on the right wears the beard of Osiris. They are both wearing the upper crown of Egypt with the Cobra Ureaus on the front. The Cobras breath would repel the Pharaohs' enemies.

Pharaoh
Pharaoh is the word we use today for the Kings of ancient Egypt. But the word Pharaoh means 'Great House' and only came into use during the new kingdom.
It was probably first used by Tuthmosis III and referred to the King's palace and his house, being the house of the two lands, Upper and Lower Egypt.

A day in the life of the Pharaoh

Everyday life for the Pharaoh was regulated by a precise ceremony and was often organised down to the last detail.

Pharaohs rose early and took prayers. After this they would be bathed and shaved by the barber. They would then be dressed in a loincloth, which displayed their rank. The Pharaoh would always wear a crown, of which he had many types and he chose the one suitable for the day's chores.

He would then put on his jewellery and often wore sandals, a privilege of the upper class.

During the day the Pharaoh concentrated on ruling, frequently being informed as to what was going on in the country. He listened to requests and dictated decisions. His scribes would write these down as records.

The most important duty was to serve the Gods. This was done by building and restoring temples, sancturies, statues and obelisks.

Every day the Pharaoh and his priests would visit a temple where in the middle sanctuary stood the effigy of a God. There would be a series of rising steps through each room and depending on your status you could only go so far, with the last room only being entered by the Pharaoh. He would then clean the effigy with ointments, dress it and make offerings, then leave the room walking backwards and sweeping his foot prints away. The Pharaoh never turned his back on a God.

Note

The Greeks gave most Pharaohs different names to their birth or throne one and some may even be known by three names. Examples being the builders of the great Pyramids of Giza.

Khufu ———— Cheops
Khafra ———— Kkephren
Menkaura ———— Mycerinus

I have used their Egyptian names, which should be more familiar.

Cartouches

The Pharaoh's five names

The Cartouche takes its name from the French word for a gun cartridge, as this is what the Napoleon army thought the symbol resembled.

The Ancient Egyptians called it a Shenu and it represented a ring of rope folded and knotted at the bottom. This signified encircling protection and placing the Pharaohs name inside indicated his power over the whole world.

Of the King's five names only his birth and throne name (given when he was crowned King) would ever appear in a cartouche.

It is believed that Snefru, the first king of the 4th dynasty, started the use of the cartouche.

Above: A fine example of a cartouche from a pillar at Kom Ombo temple.

The Pharaoh's five names.

From the middle kingdom the Pharaoh was given five names. Firstly his birth name, then four others when he became the King. Let's use Tutankhamun to show an example.

Birth name.
Tutankhamun. Son of Re, Living image of Amun.
Throne name.
Nesu-bity. King of upper and lower Egypt.
Golden Horus name.
Wetjes-Khau sehetep-netjeru. He who displays the regalia of Gods.
Nebti name.
Nefer-hepu segereh-tawy sehetep-netjeru nebu. Keeper of laws who rules two lands.
Horus name.
Ka-nakht tut- mesut. Strong bull.

The Pharaoh's Army

Chariots and Weapons

For much of its history Ancient Egypt did not have a large permanent army, but many men could always be called upon to fight and protect against invaders. Ancient Egypt had natural defences with deserts each side, the Mediterranean to the north and river cataracts *(rapids)* south.

There was, however, always a regiment of highly trained royal guards. It was around the New Kingdom that a strong professional army developed, with foot soldiers, charioteers and commanders. During this period some of the soldiers became Pharaohs, having been generals and supreme commanders such as Ramasses I. Life as a soldier was not easy, being paid very little and hoping for a share in the spoils of war.

The War chariots were very fast, travelling faster than foot soldiers and carrying two men; one as a driver that would carry a shield to protect both men and the other an archer. The ride would have been very bumpy as they had two spoked wheels fixed to an axle, a wooden chassis with wooden and leather sides.

In open battle the chariot was very effective, when advancing fast straight towards the enemy at high speeds they were hard to stop. The best defence was to dig trenches or bring down the horses.

Right: Six chariots were found in the tomb of Tutankhamun including this one in Cairo museum. Covered in gems and precious stones it was more than likely for daily use or even ceremonial instead of battle. Five of the six were restorable and articles such as whips and harnesses were found near to the chariots.

The old and middle kingdom soldiers were poorly equipped, and it was not until the new kingdom that the quality of weapons and equipment become superior to their enemies. They had the chariot, shields of wood and animal skins, helmets, bows, chain mail tunics, axes and the Khepesh sword.

Tutankhamen's Khepesh sword.

Narmer

0 Dynasty.

Little is known of the rulers of this period, except the last one, Narmer. With the increasing differences between Lower and Upper Egypt, he gained control by beheading the top rulers and uniting Egypt. This, in a way, could make him one of the most important pharaohs of all.

Narmers Palette is the oldest record of a united Ancient Egypt. In the top scene of the Palette far right, Narmer follows four flag-bearers towards rows of his beheaded enemies. The lowest scene shows him as a rampaging bull, knocking down the city walls of his enemy and crushing them.
The Palette (right) shows Narmer about to behead a captive. Notice the two crowns he wears are showing him as the complete ruler of a united Egypt.

Aha

1st Dynasty
Aha. (3032-3000 BC)
With the new founding of a unified Egypt, the monarchy had also now gained a social political role. This began to be shown in the development of new tomb architecture. Aha, son of Narmer and first ruler of the new Dynasty, shows in his tomb evidence of a custom used throughout this Dynasty. A custom of burying members of the royal household (such as servants) in nearby tombs. These people were in fact killed at the time of the Pharaoh's funeral.

2nd Dynasty
Ninetjer (2810-2767 BC)
Ninetjer was the third king of the 2nd Dynasty and took Memphis as his capital. He was famous for festivals and marvellous temples and ruled for almost 43 years.

Djoser

3rd Dynasty (2668-2649 BC) *Beginning of Old Kingdom*

The oldest and largest cemetery in Egypt, Saqqara, holds the step Pyramid of Djoser, the very first Pyramid and believed by many to be the first stone building in the world. The tomb consists of six courses rising 60 metres and has a base of 107 x 123 metres.

Below: Bust of Djoser.

Imhotep

The step Pyramid of Djoser above was the work of Imhotep, the Pharaoh's architect, vizier, priest and doctor. Together they brought about a new method of working stones to suit architectural plans, whose forms gave shape to Egypt. With the unification of Egypt, the nomadic Kings of Upper Egypt were more settled. Each King had to build his own burial place to watch over his people. The funerary complex of Djoser was surrounded by a 10 metre high wall (*above*). There were 14 doors in the wall but only one was an actual entrance, the rest were fakes.

See page 55 for more on step Pyramid.

Snefru

4th Dynasty (2589-2566 BC)

Snefru was considered one of the great Pharaohs of Egypt. The founder of the 4th Dynasty, he was an excellent administrator who strengthened the image of Pharaohs. He was also a warrior King.
Snefru also began the building of the burial site at Dahshur on a large scale. His first Pyramid was considered to be too far from his palace, and building stopped during the 13th year of his reign. The new structure was to be the first non-step Pyramid but the angle was too steep due to miscalculation and after cracks appeared the angle was changed about 50 metres above ground level. This is now known as the bent Pyramid (*below left*).

For safety reasons the project was abandoned and using new angles Snefru built the first smooth sided Pyramid. The white limestone casing has long since eroded exposing the red stone beneath. This is now known as the red Pyramid and is the first true Pyramid.

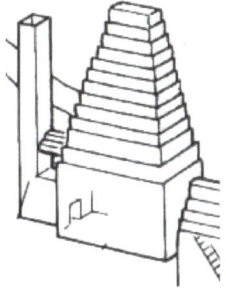

Above Right: This picture shows the impressive corbelling used to reduce loads in the burial chamber of the Red Pyramid.
Left: This detail shows the corbelling over the burial chamber in the bent Pyramid.

Khufu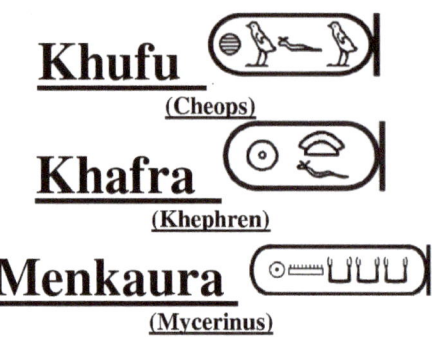
(Cheops)
Khafra
(Khephren)
Menkaura
(Mycerinus)

4th Dynasty (2589-2566 BC)

Khufu was the builder of the Great Pyramid, the only one of the Seven Wonders of the World still standing. However, little is known about him and the only surviving image is a small ivory figure found at the temple of Abydos. A pit beside the Pyramid contained the remains of his royal ship, in which the Pharaoh would have travelled to the afterlife. Now restored it shows remarkable workmanship.

Below: The tiny 3 inch ivory figure of Khufu wearing the red crown of Lower Egypt. His right hand holds a flail and his name is on the throne next to his legs.
Right: The Royal ship of Khufu.

Khafra was the son of Khufu and builder of the second Pyramid. His Pyramid has remains of the white limestone on top, most of which was removed over years for buildings in the area. It is believed the head of the Sphinx is an image of Khafra, but there is no proof of this.

Menkaura was the son of Khafra and builder of the third and smallest of the Great Pyramids. This was probably due to the hardship and drain of resources that occurred during the building of the first two Great Pyramids.   (See page 53 for more on Pyramids)

Userkaf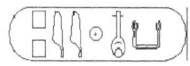

5th Dynasty (2498-2491 BC)

Userkaf was the founder of the 5th Dynasty. His wife, Queen Khentkaues, was of Royal blood. Historians say that Userkaf married her to align himself with the Royal line. Unfortunately his reign is not well documented, but he built a marvellous pyramid at Saqqara. His architecture and decoration demonstrates the artistic glory of the era. The pyramid was designed to act as a chapel for offerings and as a mortuary temple for the King. The temple court has square granite columns in all the corners and some beautiful reliefs on the walls. Two of the temple's busts were recovered recently.

Right: Bust of Userkaf

Pepi II

6th Dynasty (2278-2184) *End of the old Kingdom*

The 5th King of this Dynasty, he began his reign at the age of 6 and continued until he was 94, the longest reign ever. His father, Pepi I, died when he was young and with the help of officials, his mother maintained stability of the Kingdom until he was older. In later life however, he showed more interest in his funeral duties than concern of the Kingdom. Egypt needed a younger ruler. Expeditions of trade and conquests were met with resistance and external trouble began.

Right: Statue of Pepi II with his mother, Ankhnesmerire.

Mentuhotep I

11th Dynasty (2060-2010BC) *Beginning of the Middle Kingdom*

From the 8th to the 11th Dynasty there was a lot of struggle between north and south Egypt. Most of the Kings of this Dynasty ruled only in Thebes, they were in constant conflict with the Kings of the North. Mentuhotep I seized back the Memphis crown around the 14th year of his reign; this united the two lands again and he continued to reign for 50 years.
This was the beginning of the Middle Kingdom.

Left: A wooden statue of the seated King, Mentuhotep I, found in a chamber beneath his temple tomb.
The uniting of the lands once more saw peace and prosperity return to Egypt. Mentuhotep reigned for 50 years, a good length of time when most Pharaohs died young.

12th –18th Dynasty

This was a time of many conflicts in Egypt. The stronger Pharaohs ruled in the 12th Dynasty, such as Senusret I and Amenemhet II.
Egypt was united until around the 13th Dynasty ruler, Neferhotep I. Egypt then divided into smaller territories until the 18th Dynasty, the New Kingdom.

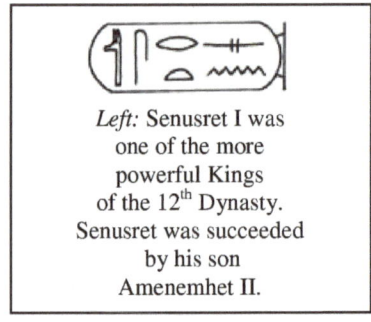

Left: Senusret I was one of the more powerful Kings of the 12th Dynasty. Senusret was succeeded by his son Amenemhet II.

The New Kingdom

1570-1070 BC 18th Dynasty

The New Kingdom was arguably the greatest period in Ancient Egyptian history. Some of the most powerful and influential Pharaohs ruled during this period and Egypt saw a rise in art, literature, wealth and the building of wonderful temples. This era is now known as the golden age.

Tuthmosis III (1504-1450 BC)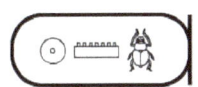

Tuthmosis II only had one illegitimate son. After his death, his wife Hatshepsut ruled for 15 years and the young Tuthmosis III was powerless. On her death he finally came to power and years of frustration had made him bitter. Regarded as one of the greatest pharaohs in history, he owes his reputation to his skill as a great military leader.

Tuthmosis III inspired fear. When he attacked the lands now known as Israel, the victory was so great that Egypt's other enemies; the Hittites, Babylonians and Assyrians chose to surrender.

When he occupied an enemy country, he would not destroy it. The rulers of that country would be taken to Egypt and taught its ways. They would then be allowed back to their country under his protection. This clever policy enabled Egypt to become rich. He also allowed his son (Amenhotep) to take part in affairs, therefore ensuring that after his death his succession passed smoothly.

This scene on the wall of the temple of Amun-Ra, Karnak, shows the king smiting his enemies.

Hatshepsut

!8th Dynasty (1498-1483BC)

Although married to Tuthmosis II, Hatshepsut was not the mother of his son, Tuthmosis III. Although his real mother was a young woman from the harem, Hatshepsut began to govern for the young pharaoh. But she ordered herself crowned pharaoh and adopted the royal name limited only to kings. She managed to bring 22 years of peace to Egypt, with successful trading explorations to the land of Punt (thought to be what is now known as Somalia) she was also an accomplished builder. Her most splendid temple is Deir el-bahari *(see page50)*, in the Valley of the Kings. This was the burial place of herself and her father, Tuthmosis I.
Her husband Tuthmosis II was actually her half brother.
After she died, Tuthmosis III had been waiting so long to be crowned that he hated her and had her name erased from wherever it could be seen.

Left: The carvings on the right above this doorway show two cartouches of Tuthmosis III. His throne name on top and birth name below right. The left carvings of Hatshepsut's cartouches have been removed. The throne name partly damaged, the birth name completely erased.

Above: Part of wall relief showing boats arriving at Punt.
Above right: Bust of Hatshepsut.

Akhenaten
Amenhotep IV

18th Dynasty (1350-1334 BC)

When the young Amenhotep IV came to the throne the priesthood of Amun had become very wealthy. The new Pharaoh was worried about their influence and power. Amenhotep dared to challenge them and a religious tradition thousands of years old. He changed his name to Akhenaten (*living spirit of Aten*) and built a new capital at Tell el-amarna (*see page 41*). He replaced all the old Gods with one all-powerful God Aten, The sun God. Although a sickly King he was a strong ruler that closed temples and dispersed the priesthood.

Akhenaten had several wives, but the most famous was Nefertiti. They had 6 children which were all believed to be girls, as this is all she is ever seen with in wall paintings and carvings. One of these was Ankhesenamun (*see Tutankhamun p76*). Akhenatens new religion only lasted as long as his reign. Although the reason for his death is unknown, it is without doubt that the old religions returned and all of his temples were abandoned to the sands of time.

Right: This sand stone Statue of Akhenaten shows the King's unusual physique and has lead to many debates about the King's illness and physical appearance. On his death, Smenkhare (thought to be his younger brother) reigned for 2 years.

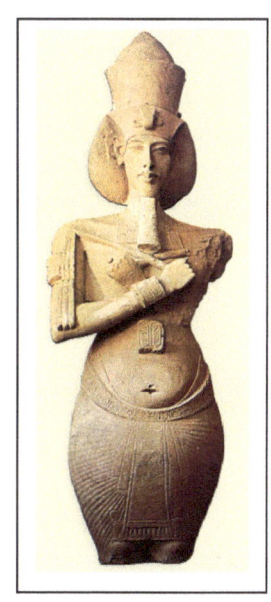

At various times through Ancient Egypt's history, Pharaohs would have lists of previous Kings carved on walls in temples to honour their ancestors. The best preserved is the list made by Seti I (Father of Ramesses II). The rulers of the Amarna period, however, are missing. Akhenaten, Tutankhamun and Ay are not listed, probably because of their religious reforms.

Left: A bust of Nefertiti found at Tell el-Amarna in 1912. Nefertiti was Akhenaten's chief wife. She was powerful and influential and often became involved in politics. She is often shown in carvings as her husband's equal. However around 1340 BC she seems to just disappear along with any records of her. Her burial place has never been discovered.

Tutankhamun
Tutankhaten

18th Dynasty (1334-1325 BC)

Maybe it's because his tomb was found only recently compared with others, but when Howard Carter discovered the burial place in 1922 he secured a place in history for the young forgotten King.

His exact identity and actual parents are unclear, but it is certain that he grew up in the court of Akhenaten at Amarna. His mother is believed to be one of Akhenaten's wives called Kiya.

He came to the throne at the age of 9, probably while under the care and influence of his stepmother Nefertiti and was married to Ankhesenamun, the daughter of Nefertiti and Akhenaten.

The priests took advantage of the boy King's age and set about replacing the religion of Aten enforced by his father. It was most probably on the advice of others that the old religions of Amun returned and thus the boy King's name was changed from Tutankhaten to Tutankhamun.

His death at such a young age, around 18, is still a mystery. X-rays carried out on the body in modern times have shown a small trauma to the head that was probably the cause of a blow. This has led to speculation of a fall from a chariot or even murder. Tutankhamun died without having any children for heirs, but mummified bodies of two stillborn girls were found beside the body of the King.

Left: Tutankhamun's sarcophagus in his tomb known as KV62, Valley of the Kings. He was the only Pharaoh discovered to be left to rest in his tomb in modern times.
During my second trip to Egypt in 2012, on entering the tomb it was with overwhelming excitement that I found the boy King had been removed and placed in a climate controlled glass case in the tomb for all to see. Face to face with the young Pharaoh, my childhood dream comes true.

Tutankhamun

Treasures & Burial chamber

In 1917 Howard Carter, with the finance of Lord Carnarvon, was in the Valley of the Kings working on the tombs of the Ramesses when he discovered twelve jars bearing the name of Tutankhamun. He searched for a tomb but without success. In 1922 Carter persuaded Carnarvon to finance another dig. One morning on the 4th November a young servant water carrier for Carter found a step cut into the rocks. The rest is history.

The steps led down to a sealed doorway and behind this was a corridor leading to a second sealed door. Once opened Carter found the antechamber which contained hundreds of items and food for the Pharaoh in the afterlife, including bread, wine, and even his chariots. Two more sealed doors lead to another chamber of the King's belongings and the burial chamber.

Inside the burial chamber Carter found four wooden box shrines gilded in gold. There was hardly space to move around chamber but once the doors of the first shrine were opened a further three were found inside, each smaller than the other. Inside the last one was the stone sarcophagus, which contained two wooden coffins each gilded in gold and a third made of solid gold weighing a staggering 1100 kilograms. Inside was the body of Tutankhamun and the golden death mask (page 78).

Above: The solid gold coffin inner coffin of Tutankhamun.

The lavish gold shrines, coffin, and golden mask found suggest that like most Pharaohs the burial arrangements were started as soon as he became King, or even when he was born. However, because of his early death it is believed that the tomb was actually for someone of lesser status. Maybe a King's advisor, as this was usual custom. The tomb compared with others in the valley is far too small for a royal burial.

Items from the tomb of Tutankhamun

Probably the most famous Egyptian artefact ever found is the golden death mask of Tutankhamun. Weighing 25lb (11kg) and made of gold, it is thought to represent the young Pharaoh himself. He wears the royal nemes headdress inlaid with precious metal and stones, which were considered divine materials; Lapis Lazuli, Turquoise, Quartz and Gold that represented the skin of the Gods. The vulture goddess Nekhbet, the symbol of Upper Egypt and the erect cobra Uraeus of Lower Egypt can be seen on the forehead of the mask. These were the protectors of royalty. The beard of Osiris beneath the chin is a symbol of immortality. This would have been false as the Pharaoh was clean shaven.

The Hieroglyphs on the back identified the King with different Gods and is from the Book of the Dead. Seeing this mask for myself in 2012 was a very moving and personal moment.

Above left. The biggest of shrines can be seen followed by the smaller.
Left: The Canopic jars (*see page 17*)
Above: The solid gold throne chair shows the young King and his wife,

Horemheb

18th Dynasty (1321- 1293 BC)

Horemheb became a general in the army during the reign of Akenaten. He was loyal to the King, but only through ambition and only while the King lived. Horemheb had no trouble with changing his beliefs and loyalty to the new boy Pharaoh Tutankhamun.

He was made the King's deputy and honoured with the title of Prince. This may have caused conflict at the time as it placed Horemheb above other ranking royal advisors.

With the death of the young King, Horemheb was probably now the most powerful man in Egypt. Yet the throne was passed to Tutankhamun's most trusted advisor Ay.

Ay ruled for 4 years and by now Horemheb was so powerful that no one contested his right to succeed. During his 27-year reign time was devoted to restoring the religion of Amon. The name of Akhenaten was removed from temples and the city of Tell-El Armarna was destroyed.

He now considered himself direct successor of the 18th Dynasty. Unfortunately he had little in common with his predecessors as he was not related by blood or marriage and is believed to have had no heirs. Horemheb passed his throne on to his most trusted and close friend Ramesses. Known as Ramesses I, this was the start of the 19th Dynasty.

Below: Horemheb makes offerings to the Gods on his tomb wall.
Right: Ay carries out the ceremony of opening the mouth on the mummy of Tutankhamun. Ay is wearing the blue war helmet of a Pharaoh that suggests he is already the new King.

19th Dynasty

Seti I (1291-1278 BC)

The 19th Dynasty began with Ramesses I, but his reign was short, (probably about two years) and he was succeeded by his son Seti I. Seti's reign spanned 13 years and saw a high point in art and culture. Some of the huge tasks undertaken include the massive Hypostyle Hall at the temple of Amun at Karnak (*See page 42*).
The quality of carvings and reliefs on his temple walls are rarely equalled throughout Egypt. His own tomb in the valley of kings is the finest, with superior workmanship. The detail below shows the astronomical ceiling in the burial chamber.
His Queen, Tuya, was from the same military class and background to himself. She outlived him by many years, into the reign of their son, Ramesses II.
Seti I's mummy was found in the great royal cache (*place for hiding treasures or supplies*) at Deir el-bahari (*see page 50*). Documentation and records of the mummy show various moves from its original place.

Left: Statue of a kneeling Set I.
Below: The Tomb of Seti I was the earliest one to have this shaped ceiling. Painted dark blue to represent the night sky with yellow figures that represent stars of the Northern constellation and planets known to the ancient Egyptians, including Venus and Mars.

Ramesses II

19th Dynasty (1279-1212 BC)

As ancient Egypt's best known and one of the longest lived Pharaohs, Ramesses succeeded his father at the age of 25 and reigned over 67 years, outliving many of his children. He had eight wives and records show he fathered over 100 sons and daughters. His favourite wife was Nefertari, for whom he built the amazing temple at Abu Simbel *(see pages 37)* and ordered the construction of her tomb in the Valley of the Queens *(page59)*. At the start of his reign Egypt was a troubled land because of outside powers. In the 5th year of his reign he led the biggest Egyptian army ever seen. 20,000 men in four divisions of 5000 marched to the boarders of Syria against the Hittities, people of modern day Turkey.

This was the first ever-recorded battle and took place in the city of Kadesh. It was a major trade route and was first conquered by his father Seti 1, but after his army withdraw the city fell into the hands of the Hittities.

Ramesses led his division of 5,000 men, known as Amun division, into the first attack. He had miscalculated the size of the Hittities army that numbered 37,000; many of his men were killed and he became isolated. The story on many of his temple walls depicts that Ramesses then single handidly beat off his enemy. This is highly unlikely and in fact he was saved by the arrival of the other divisions that attacked the Hittities from behind. There was however no outright victory and a ceasefire was called.

Under his reign Egypt flourished, trade with outside merchants grew and Ramesses set about showing his power and wealth by building some of the finest and biggest temples in Egypt. No other Pharaoh built so many temples and statues.

Right:
Two of the four 20 metre high statues of Ramesses at the entrance to the temple at Abu Simbel. A demonstration of power over his enemies.

Ramesses was certainly the most prolific builder of all the Pharaohs. His greatest achievement was the temple of Abu Simbel.
His own tomb in the Valley of the Kings was robbed by raiders in about 1000BC, but his mummy was rescued by priests and hidden.
It was discovered in 1875. Ramesses was about 90 when he died.

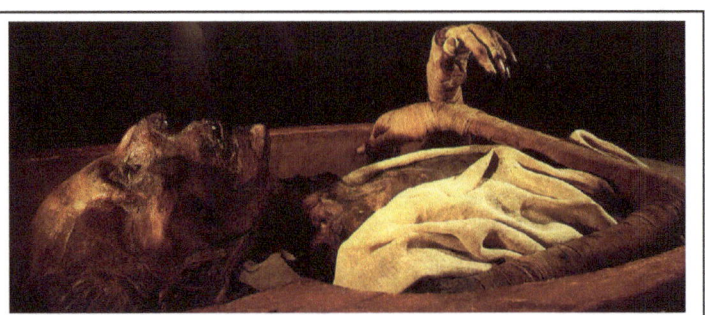

Left: the mummified body of Ramesses II as it is now in the Cairo museum.

The picture on the left is a colossal black granite statue of the Pharaoh wearing the white crown of Upper Egypt. It stands in the complex at Luxor.
The right picture shows the size of the two figures of the King flanking his Queen at the temple of Nefertari at Abu Simbel.

Ramesses & Nefertari

Ramesses had two principal wives, Nefertari and Istnofret, but Nefertari was always the Queen while she lived. At Abu Simbel on the temple dedicated to her she is shown as the Goddess Hathor and stands at the same height as the King beside her. This was unusual for these times and is maybe a sign of his love for her. This dedication can also be seen in the building of her beautiful tomb in the Valley of the queens.

Little is known of both wives and Nefertari died around the 24th year of Ramesses' reign. Istnofret became Queen but died around 10 years later.

Above left: The figure standing between the legs of this colossal statue of Ramesses at the temple of Karnak is thought to be his daughter Bint-Anath. This is a Syrian name of the times and meant 'daughter of Anath'. She may have been named due to his new alliance with the Hittities.

Above right: The author stands in front of the impressive statues of Nefertari at the entrance to her temple at Abu Simbel. Shown as the Goddess Hathor, notice her headdress is as high if not slightly higher than the King himself. Surely a sign of his love and her own importance and input of affairs as Queen.

Queen Twosret

19th Dynasty (1187-1183 BC)

Ramesses II's 13th son Merneptah (1212-02) succeeded his father but was already into his sixties. He carried on to be a strong leader like his father and crushed revolts from Syria, Libyans and Nubians. He also continued his father's treaty with the Hittites, even sending them grain in times of famine. It is not understood why, but when Merneptah died the son of a lesser queen became king and not the crown prince. His name was Amenmesses and he reigned for 4 years. (1202-1199) His successor was Seti II, (1199-93) who could have been crown prince. Evidence for this is seen in the fact that Seti had his predecessors' names removed from monuments and added his own. Seti II outlived his eldest son so when he died his younger son Siptah (1193-87) was crowned Pharaoh. Siptah was only a minor and so the older and most important Queen at the time, Twosret, ruled in her stepson's name. Finally she declared herself Pharaoh and used the full Pharonic title that Hatshepsut had done 300 years earlier.

Left: Pillar from the tomb of Twosret.

Women Pharaohs

The first woman Pharaoh was Queen Merneith (2950BC) from the 1st Dynasty. Nitiqret (2184-81) is found at the end of the 6th Dynasty. The end of the 12th Dynasty saw the reign of Queen Sobekneferu (1785-82). The reign of Hatshepsut (1479-58) saw a flourishing period for Egypt. Twosret only reigned for two years and little is known about this time.
The last Queen was Cleopatra VII, (51-30 BC).

20th Dynasty

New Kingdom Ends

Ramesses III (1182-51 BC) To Ramesses XI (1098-70 BC)

The 20th Dynasty was begun by Setnakhte, however very little is known about him. His son Ramesses III started a line of no fewer than 9 pharaohs with the same name. Ramess III came to the throne in 1185BC and was to be the last of the truly great Egyptian pharaohs. The outside world was in turmoil and a great movement of people seeking new lands and homes was about to arrive on the shores of Egypt.

The first sign of trouble came in the 5th year of his reign. The Libyans joined with two other tribes, the Meshwesh and the Seped. Attracted by the fertile lands of the Delta they forced their way into the west, but the Egyptian army was too strong for them and most were slaughtered. This win was, for a while, a good warning to bordering countries.

In year 8 things became increasingly worse in the Middle East. There had been bad harvests and a great surge of people were on the move and trying to settle. The mass was made up of different tribes, which soon became a huge force on the move. Together they were known as the sea people.

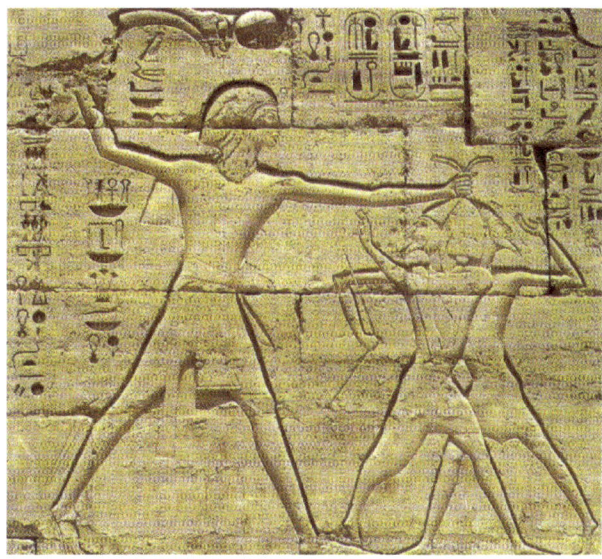

On the walls of Ramesses III mortuary temple at Medinet Habu, is an illustrated account of his fight against the sea people. The written account is on the outer walls and is the longest hieroglyphic inscription known. The invasion was halted by the Egyptian army, as was another attempt in year 11 of his reign.
Left: Ramesses III seizes the enemy by the hair ready to strike.

Because the invasions were a mass of people on the move, they had all their possessions with them. The second invasion itself left over 2000 dead and all their belongings would go to the treasury of Amun.
This built up the wealth of the priesthood of Amun and would have a disastrous consequence in the next Dynasty.

The Power of the Pharaoh Weakens

The Third Intermediate Period 1069-525BC
The Late Period 525-332BC

With the end of Ramesses III's 31 year reign came the end of the Egyptian Pharaohs' greatness. Only some 61 years before had seen the era of the great Ramesses II. In the next 71 years no fewer than 7 rulers would have a brief spell on the throne; Ramesses IV to Ramesses XI. Papyrus documents show that even during the last years of Ramesses XI reign civil war raged on and off in the region of Thebes.

The Priests had become very wealthy under Ramesses III and now owned a large majority of temples, ships and manufacturing. With the Pharaohs ruling in the North and occupied by conflicts it was an easy move for the high priest at the time, Herihor (1080-1074 BC) to place himself above the last Ramesses King and become ruler in the South.

Egypt was no longer a self contained country and the next stage of its history would see the influence of outside civilizations. This would be known as the Third intermediate period. The greatness Egypt had known in the Old, Middle and New Kingdom was coming to an end.

Third Intermediate Period

The high priests continued to rule in Thebes until 945 BC but with the division of Egypt a new city arose in the North of the Delta called Tanis. The first Pharaoh was Smendes 1 (1069-1043BC) and this was the beginning of the 21st Dynasty. The country was now divided but old traditions were still followed and the Pharaohs and priests still continued with inter marriages. This may have been a careful move on both sides to cement alliances.

22nd Dynasty (Libyan) 945-860 BC.
The first Pharaoh of this era was a Libyan leader called Sheshonq I (945-924 BC). He was married into the throne to a princess of Psusennes II, the last Pharaoh of the 21st dynasty. Sheshonq was a strong leader and he set up his sons in high places such as General of the armies and was able to control the country. Tactics like this had not been seen since the days of Ramesses III.

23rd & 24th Dynasties

These two Dynasties both began before the end of the 22nd Dynasty. In the 8th year of the reign of Sheshonq III (825-773 BC) there was a break away in the city of Leontopolis by Prince Pedibastet (818-793 BC).

The 24th Dynasty consisted of only two Kings. The first, Tefnakht (727-720 BC) of Sais realized the new threat of a Nubian invasion from the south. He organized a coalition between all the Northern Kings to hold back the Nubians. The two armies met at Herakleopolis where the coalition surrendered to the Nubian King Piankhi (747-716 BC). However the Northern Kings were spared and allowed to return and govern their own cities.

25th Dynasty (Nubian & Kushite) 747-656 BC

The Nubian invasion was probably not such a shock to the Egyptians as the Nubians had already taken on some of the Egyptian religions and beliefs. It was not long before Piankhi restored the supremacy of Amun. He even had his sister enter the priesthood of Amun and given the title of Divine Adoratrice of Amun. She took control of the priests at Thebes.

> Divine Adoratrice:
> This was an Egyptian title for the chief priestess. Holding this title gave her the greatest influence over the priests, even overseeing the crowning of new Pharaohs. She would even have a big part in the affairs and economy of the country.

At his coronation in 747BC Piankhi invested himself with the names of two of the greatest Egyptian Pharaohs, Tuthmosis III and Ramesses II.

26th Dynasty (664-525 BC)

Towards the end of the 25th Dynasty King Taharqa (690-664 BC) was in constant threat from near eastern powers of Assyrians. When they captured Memphis, Taharqa retreated south. After his death his cousin Tanutamun (664-656 BC) became King and marched North again but the Assyrian King Ashurbanipal acted swiftly and defended Memphis with success.

The task of controlling the princes and Kings of Egypt was given to the first King of the 26th Dynasty, Psamtik I (664-610 BC). Egypt became more stable under his power and old beliefs and religions returned. The gradual collapse of the Assyrian power however saw new threats from other nations. One of the biggest was that of the Babylonians and Persians.

27th Dynasty (First Persian) 525-404 BC

Within a year of being crowned the last Pharaoh of the 26th Dynasty, Psamtik III (526-525 BC) had to fight off attacks from the Persians, already skilled at war after their battles against the Greeks. The inexperienced King was no match and was captured at Memphis. This led to the 27th Dynasty and the first Persian Period. The second King of the 27th Dynasty, Darius I (521-486 BC) took most interest in the affairs and running of Egypt. But it was still a period of many revolts. The Persians were still at war with the Greeks and the Egyptians took advantage of their distractions. An Egyptian prince named Inaros of Heliopolis used Greek mercenaries for a revolt in 454BC. He was defeated and executed.

28th Dynasty (404-399 BC)

Another Prince who had been fighting the Persians for 6 years was more successful. With the death of the last Persian King, Amyrtaeus declared himself Pharaoh and managed to rule as far as Aswan. He was the only Pharaoh of this Dynasty and little is known of him.

The Enemies of Ancient Egypt

Nubians
Nubians were people of southern and northern Sudan. They settled along the banks of the Nile around the area of Aswan.

Kushites
The Kingdom of Kush was an ancient African Kingdom in what is now known as Sudan.

Babylonians
Babylonians were an ancient culture based in central Mesopotamia (Present day Iraq). Their capital city was Babylon. They were often in conflict with Assyrians of Northern Mesopotamia.

Persians
Persians are traced back to an ancient Iranian people. The origins of Iranian/Persian people were originally nomadic.

Libyans
From earlier times, Libyans and other Mediterranean people, who settled mostly in the delta (northern Egypt), had constituted a substantial part of the Egyptian army as mercenaries. They were most likely the descendants of captured prisoners or even settlers who had been granted land of their own on the condition of their military service.

29th – 30th & 31st Dynasty (399-332 BC)

The 29th and 30th Dynasty saw again the reign of 5 Egyptian Pharoahs, but each was under constant threat from the Persians.

Nectanebo1 (380-362 BC)

The first of two Kings of the 29th dynasty, Nectanebo I started the last of native Egyptian Kings. He spent most of his years in power defending his Kingdom against Persian attacks. He did however manage to erect many new temples and restore some of the older ones. He was the builder of the 2.7 kilometre line of human headed rams known as the Avenue of Sphinx between Luxor and Karnak. *(Below)*

Nectanebo II (360-343 BC) was the last Pharaoh of the 30th Dynasty. He again brought some stability to Egypt with the help of the old Gods. He built and refurbished many temples and reinstalled the value of a Pharaoh. But in 343BC Egypt was again under attack from the Persians. Even with thousands of Greek mercenaries Nectanebo was defeated and fled to Nubia. The Persians ruled once more in the 31st Dynasty (343-332 BC), the second Persian period.

> *With the end of his reign in 343 BC Nectanebo II became the last of the Egyptian Pharaohs. An Egyptian would not rule again for 2295 years when General Neguib took over in the 1952 revolt.*

Alexander the Great

Alexander III (332-323 BC)

When the Macedonian king, Phillip II died, his 20 year old son Alexander continued his father's attack on the struggling Persian Empire. He marched through Asia Minor and entered Egypt where he defeated Darius III, the last Persian Pharaoh of the 31st Dynasty.
The Egyptians saw Alexander as their saviour and in Memphis he was crowned Pharaoh, restoring the Pharaonic line. Alexander went on to restore many temples that had been destroyed or ruined by the Persians. On the mouth of the Delta he founded the first and greatest of many cities to bear his name, Alexandria. But Alexander only actually stayed in Egypt for 1 year. He left in 331 BC to continue his fight against the Persians. He was never to return alive.

The city of Alexandria had become a wealthy trading point, but it had also opened Egypt to a bigger influence from the outside world. Egypt was no longer the self contained haven safe within the Nile valley.

Alexander died of a fever in 323 BC and was succeeded by his half brother and then his own son Alexander IV. A childhood friend of Alexander the Great and later General of his armies called Lagus had a son, Ptolemy. When Alexander IV died, Lagus placed his son on the throne of Egypt. He was Ptolemy I and started the Ptolemaic Dynasty.

Above: Alexander the Great as Pharaoh makes an offering to the God Amun-Min.
Outer wall, temple of Amun at Luxor.

Ptolemaic Period (305-30 BC)

Ptolemy I

Alexander the Great's body was to be taken from Babylon back to Macedonia and buried with his father, but Ptolemy I took the body back to Memphis where Alexander had been crowned. However, it is believed his final resting place was in the city of Alexandria. His tomb has never been found and it could be under the sea due to coastlines erosion over the years.

All the rulers of this period took the name of Ptolemy and they were the last Dynasty of Ancient Egypt before the Roman conquest in 30 BC. They took on the old ways and religions of Ancient Egypt, even building some magnificent temples for the old Gods.

Egypt did well for a time under the Ptolemies but there were many conflicts and corruption amongst their families. Ptolemy VIII killed his own son and Ptolemy XI married his own aunt, Queen Berenice, to become King. He then had her murdered but the Queen had been very popular and he himself was hung only 19 days into his reign.

Above: The temple of Horus at Edfu. Started by Ptolemy III it is one of the finest preserved temples in Egypt.

Queen Cleopatra (VII)

Cleopatra (36-30 BC)

Egypt now fell under the ruling of Ptolemy XII's daughter, Cleopatra. Only 17, she was instructed to marry her elder brother PtolemyXIII. He was only 10 years old but the young boy struggled to seize full power and tried to have Cleopatra murdered. She escaped to Syria after being warned by loyalists. Around this time the Roman Emperor Julius Caesar arrived in Egypt pursuing his fleeing enemy Pompey, who had fled from the battle. Caesar stayed in Alexandria and in a civil war he defeated Ptolemy XIII and placed Cleopatra back on the throne. When Caesar left for battles in Asia Minor he had Cleopatra marry her younger brother Ptolemy XIV, still a child, and share the crown. By now Caesar and Cleopatra had a son, Caesarion (PtolemyXV) and together they planned to rule a new Empire on his return. Caesar never returned and was assassinated in Rome in 44 Bc. Cleopatra had her husband/brother the young Ptolemy XIV murdered and installed her son as ruler alongside herself.

Rome was now ruled by Mark Antony in the East and Octavian in the West. Mark Antony tried to use Cleopatra's wealth to finance a war, but this was a failure. He settled in Egypt and left his wife, who was sister of Octavian in Rome. Octavian was furious and charged Antony with treachery against Rome. He invaded Egypt and Antony knew he would be defeated and committed suicide. Cleopatra was no match for Octavian and believing she would be taken to Rome and displayed as a prisoner of Octavian she too committed suicide. She killed herself by the Venomous bite of a Cobra, symbol of the Goddess Wadjet and protector of the Pharaohs.

Cleopatra's death marked the end of the Pharaohs' Reign.

Right: Cleopatra and her son Caesarion make offerings to the gods at the temple of Hathor in Dendera.

Chapter 7

Page 94. Present day Egypt.
Page 95. Aswan Dam
Page 96. Acknowledgments

Present Day Egypt

The country of Egypt is in the Northeast corner of Africa and the Southwest corner of Asia. It covers an area of 1,010,000 square Kilometres (390,000Sqm) and is bordered to the North by the Mediterranean Sea, the Gaza strip and Israel to the Northeast, the Gulf of Aqaba to the East, the Red Sea to the East and South, Sudan to the South and Libya to the West.

Having been continuously inhabited since the 10th millennium BC, Egypt has one of the longest histories of any modern country. Tourism, agriculture and industry are the biggest parts of the economy, with Egypt being considered to be one of the significant cultural, political, and military influences in North Africa.

Most of Egypt's rain falls in the winter months South of Cairo. Rainfall averages only around 2 to 5 mm (0.1 to 0.2 in) per year and at intervals of many years. On a very thin strip of the northern coast the rainfall can be as high as 410 mm (16.1 in), mostly between October and March. Temperatures average between 80 and 90 °F (26.7 and 32.2 °C) in summer, and up to 109 °F (43 °C) on the Red Sea coast. Winter temperatures average between 55 and 70 °F (13 and 21 °C). A steady wind from the northwest helps lower temperatures near the Mediterranean coast.

Egyptian Food is mostly a vegetarian diet, as it relies heavily on vegetable dishes. Though food in Alexandria and the coast of Egypt uses a great deal of fish and other seafood, most Egyptian cuisine is based on foods that grow out of the ground. Meat has always been very expensive for most Egyptians, so a great number of vegetarian dishes have been developed.

Football is the most popular National sport. The Egyptian national football team won the African Cup of Nations seven times, including three times in a row in 2006, 2008, and 2010.

Transport in Egypt is centered in Cairo and largely follows the pattern of settlement along the Nile. The main line of the nation's 40,800-kilometre (25,400 miles) railway network runs from Alexandria to Aswan and is operated by Egyptian National Railways. The badly maintained vehicle road network has expanded rapidly to over 21,000 miles, covering the Nile Valley and Nile Delta. The Cairo Metro in Egypt is the first of only two full-fledged metro systems in Africa and the Arab World. The system consists of three operational lines.

The flag of Egypt is a tricolour consisting of the three equal horizontal red, white, and black bands of the Arab Liberation flag dating back to the Egyptian Revolution of 1952. The flag bears Egypt's national emblem, the Eagle of Saladin centered in the white band.

Aswan Dam

The Nile levels are now controlled by the Aswan Dam. The old Dam was built by the British between 1898-1902, but by 1952 it was apparent that the Dam could not satisfy Egypt's demands because of the population explosion.

Under President Nasser, a new Dam was built 6km up stream between 1960-1971. President Nasser's request for a loan was turned down by the World Bank under pressure from America. As Egypt now had control over the Suez Canal, Nasser nationalised it to generate money for the building of the new Dam and turned to the USSR for assistance.

The build-up of water behind the Dam is called Lake Nasser. It is the biggest reservoir in the world and stretches back 500km into the Sudan. Because the Dam traps the silt, which was once deposited on the fields along the Nile, farmers now rely on fertilizers. Interestingly, the old Dam is now mainly used to generate hydroelectricity for the nearby fertilizer factory. This silt would also carry on down and be deposited along the coast were the Delta meets the Mediterranean. This coast line is now slowly corroding. It is estimated that Lake Nasser will be full of silt within 500 years.

If the dam were to burst, most of Egypt's population would be washed into the Mediterranean. Security is high after threats to bomb the Dam by Israel in 1967, 1973 and by Gadaffi in 1984.

The picture above was taken by the author standing on top of the New Dam with his back to Lake Nasser. Cameras are allowed, Videos are not.

Acknowledgments

I would like to thank the following people for their help
in the making of this book.

My partner Karen

For putting up with the endless evenings of researching,
helping with the layout and general guidance.

For supplying photos

Lauren Donovan
Cliff Major
Kay Debrincat
Sandra & Ray Ellis

For proof reading and advice

Karen Donovan
Kayleigh Ellis
Greg Ellis
Tony (Dod) & Joan Jasper
Jazmin Donovan

Pictures

Back cover: Columns from the Hypostyle hall, Karnak.

The Author's partner stands in front of one of the many cruise boats on their 2012 trip to Egypt.

Head of the Sphinx, Giza

Row of statues, Luxor – Row of Ram headed Sphinx, Karnak.

2014

Index

A
Abu Gurab 36
Abu Simbel <u>37</u>, 38, 39
Acknowledgments 96
Abydos 70
Afterlife 19
Aglika 48
Aha 67
Akhenaten 37, 41, 44, <u>75</u>
Akhetaten 41
Alexander III, the Great 40, <u>90</u>
Alexander IV 90
Alexandria 24, <u>40</u>, 47
Alexandria, the Lighthouse 40
Amenemhet II 72
Amenhotep II 18
Amenhotep III 58
Amenhotep IV 41
Amenmesses 84
Ammut 19
Amun 42, <u>44</u>
Amun-Ra 63
Amyrtaeus 88
Ankh 20
Ankhesenamun 75, <u>76</u>, 78
Antony, Mark 92
Anubis 11, 15, <u>16</u>, 19
Artisans 46
Armies 66
Aswan Dam 95
Aten 75
Atlantis 57
Atum <u>11</u>, 36
Avenue of Sphinx 80
Ay 75, <u>79</u>

B
Ba 19
Babylonians 87
Baraize, Emile 57
Bastet 33
Belzoni, Giovanni 37
Bent Pyramid 69
Berenice (Queen) 91

Biga 48
Bint-Anath 83
Bouchard, Pierre-Francois 24
Brewing beer 29
Burckhadt, Jean-Louis 37
Burial sites 55

C
Caesar, Julius 40, 92
Caesarion (Ptolemy XV) 92
Cairo 8, <u>49</u>, 94
Canopic jars 15, <u>17</u>
Carnarvon, Lord 77
Carter, Howard 77
Cartouche 65
Cataracts 7
Champollion, Jean Francois 24
Chariots 66
Cleopatra (Queen) 46, <u>92</u>
Cleopatra's needle 36
Clothing 31
Colossi of Memnon 58
Counting 34

D
Darius I 88
Darius III 90
Death mask 78
Delta 7
Determinatives 23
Dier-el Bahari <u>50</u>, 74, 80
Dier-el Medina 56
Dinocrates 40
Djoser 55, <u>68</u>
Duamutef 17

E
Edfu 12, <u>46</u>, 91
Education 27
Egypt (Early) 8
Egypt (Present day) 94
El-Qurn 58
Ethiopia 7

F
Farming 29

G
Geb <u>11</u>, 36
Giza 33
Gods & Goddesses (List) 13
Gods & Goddesses (In form) 14

H
Hathor <u>12</u>, 37
Hatshepsut (Queen) 43, 50, 52, <u>74</u>
Hapy 17
Haroeris 51
Heka (Sceptre) 63
Heliopolis 36
Herihor 86
Hieroglyphs 22, <u>23</u>
Hieroglyphs (alphabet) 22
Hittites 43, 81, 83
Horemheb 44, 60, <u>79</u>
Horus <u>12</u>, 46, 63
Hygiene 32
Hypostle hall 42

I
Ideograms 23
Imhotep 47, <u>68</u>
Imsety 17
Inaros (Prince) 88
Irrigation 9
Isis <u>11</u>, 36, 48
Istnofret 83

K
Ka 19
Kadesh 81
Karnak 9, <u>42</u>, 43, 63
Khafre 53, 57, 64, <u>70</u>
Khartoum 7
Khepesh 66
Khepri 15

97

Khons 44
Khufu 53, 57, 64, 70
Kiya 76
Kom Ombo 9, 30, 34, 51
Kushites 88

L
Labourers 56
Lagus 90
Late Period (525-332BC) 86
Lotus Lake 19
Lower Egypt 8
Luxor (Thebes) 44

M
Map 6
Mastabas 55
Measuring 34
Medicine 30
Memphis 24, 47
Menkaure 53, 63, 70
Mentuhotep I 72
Merneith (Queen) 84
Merneptah 84
Montu 42
Mummification 15
Mut 42

N
Napoleon 24
Narmer 8, 67
Nectanebo I & II 89
Nefertari (Queen) 37, 45, 59, 83
Nefertiti (Queen) 75
Nekhakha (Whip) 63
Nemes headdress 32, 63
Nephthys 11
New kingdom (1570-1070BC) 73, 85
Nile (river) 7
Nileometer 7, 9
Nitiqret 84
Nubia 37
Nubian Desert 7
Nun 11
Nut 11, 36, 50

Nyuserra 36

O
Obelisk 52
Obelisk (Unfinished) 52
Old Kingdom (2686-2181BC) 68, 71
Osiris 11, 36
Ostraca 56

P
Papyrus 25, 26
Pedibastet (Prince) 87
Pepi I & II 71
Perfume 31
Persians 87
Pets 33
Pharaohs 62
    The meaning of 63
    A day in the life of 64
    Five names of 65
Philae 9, 48
Phillip II 90
Phonograms 23
Piankhi 87
Psamtik III 88
Psusennes II 86
Ptah 47
Ptolemy period 91
Ptolemy I 48, 90
Ptolemy II 40
Ptolemy III 46, 91
Ptolemy V 24
Ptolemy VIII 91
Ptolemy XI 91
Punt 74
Pyramids 53
    Construction 54

Q
Qaitbaty 40
Qebehsenuef 17

R
Ra 36, 44
Ramesses I 66

Ramesses II 23, 36, 37, 42, 43, 44, 47, 59, 81, 82, 83
Red Pyramid 69
Rosetta stone 23
Royal ship 70

S
Sarcophagus 18, 72
Schiaparelli, Ernesto 59
Scribes 25
Senusret I 36, 50, 72
Seth 19, 36
Seti I 42, 75, 80, 81
Sheshonq I 86
Shu 11, 36
Siptah 84
Smendes 86
Smenkhare 75
Snefru 65, 69
Sobek 51
Sobekneferu (Queen) 84
Solar barge 19
Sphinx 57
Step Pyramid 55
Suez Canal 6
Syria 37

T
Taharqa 87
Tanis 86
Tanutamun 87
Tefnakht 87
Tefnut 11, 36
Tel-el Amarna 41, 75
Thebes 44, 47
Third Intermediate Period (1069-525BC) 86
Tomb construction 60
Toys & games 33
Tutankhamun 17, 32, 33, 37, 44, 60, 65, 66, 76
Tuthmosis I 43
Tuthmosis III 36, 46, 50, 63, 73, 87
Twosret (Queen) 84

U
Uganda 7
United Egypt
    (The three crowns) 8
Upper Egypt 8
Uraeus 32
Userkaf 71

V
Valley of the Kings 58, 81
Valley of the Queens 59

W
Weapons 66
Wedjet Eye 12
Weighing of the heart 19

Y
Yalu (fields of) 19

Years of the Dynasties

Early 3150 – 2686 BC

The Old Kingdom 2686 – 2181 BC

The First Intermediate Period 2181 – 2040 BC
The Middle kingdom 2040 – 1782 BC
The Second Intermediate Period 1782 – 1570 BC

The New kingdom 1570 – 1070 BC

20th Dynasty Pg 85

21st, 22nd Dynasty Pg 86

23rd, 24th, 25th, 26th, Dynasty Pg 87

27th, 28th Dynasty Pg 88

29th, 30th, 31st Dynasty Pg 89

The Third Intermediate Period 1069 – 525 BC
The Late Period 525 – 332 BC
332 – 305 BC Macedonian Kings (Including Alexander the Great)
305 – 30 BC Ptolemy Dynasty

With the death of Cleopatra in 30 BC the Reign of the Pharaohs' ended.

www.ingramcontent.com/pod-product-compliance
Lightning Source LLC
Chambersburg PA
CBHW042014080426
42735CB00002B/49